The Auld Inns of

An Ayrshireman, Dane Love lives in the countryside near Cumnock. He works as a schoolteacher
at Irvine Royal Academy, but enjoys travelling
with his wife around Scotland doing research. He
is interested in all aspects of Scottish history, and
has written histories of the Ayrshire towns and
villages of Ayr, Cumnock and Auchinleck. With an
interest in genealogy, he has traced his ancestry
back to one Robin Love who fought for Bonnie
Prince Charlie at the battles of Prestonpans and
Culloden. His books include *Scottish Kirkyards*
and *Scottish Ghosts* both published by Robert
Hale.

The
Auld Inns of
Scotland

DANE LOVE

ROBERT HALE · LONDON

ISBN 0 7090 5987 6

Robert Hale Limited
Clerkenwell House
Clerkenwell Green
London EC1R 0HT

2   4   6   8   10   9   7   5   3   1

Photoset in North Wales by
Derek Doyle & Associates, Mold, Flintshire.
Printed in Great Britain by
St Edmundsbury Press Ltd, Bury St Edmunds, Suffolk.
Bound by WBC Book Manufacturers Limited,
Bridgend, Mid-Glamorgan.

Contents

Illustrations

Introduction

Some of the many differences between Scotland and England are often apparent in their inns. England has a long history of village inns which have been the focus of village life for centuries, and many survive from the fifteenth and sixteenth centuries. In Scotland things were different. In some villages the occupants of virtually every second house made and sold their own brews of ale or whisky. And if travellers required accommodation, it was the done thing for them to be put up in any house in the parish, with no charge payable for the hospitality.

In Scotland the inn as an institution probably only dates back to the seventeenth century, outside the larger towns (burghs) at least – and even then it was little more than a 'public' house where ale was sold. It was in the eighteenth century that the improvement in roads and the advent of stage-coach travel gave rise to the coaching inn, and most of the country's 'auld inns' date from this period; anything older has usually been swept away in redevelopment work, not necessarily of a recent period. Government-sponsored inn-building, unique to Scotland, also dates from the eighteenth century. The King's Houses were established in remote parts of the Highlands to allow travellers on the new military roads to obtain board and lodging – and the landlord of the Kingshouse Hotel on Rannoch Moor was even given a subsidy to keep open. New fishing communities were established, and there, too, government-backed inns were erected.

There are many old inns throughout the length and breadth of Scotland that have played a part in the country's history or have fascinating tales associated with them. This book mentions a fair selection of them – though no doubt there are hundreds more with interesting tales associated with them that have failed to reach my ears. Here we find out where the haunted inns are, and the manifestations that make rare appearances there. We find out the places that the famous sons of the country frequented – from the ubiquitous Robert Burns to Sir Walter Scott, James Hogg, Robert Louis Stevenson and a host of others. There are tales of murder and of love, of cattle drovers resting man and beast on their journeys, and of smugglers hiding their booty. In most cases the inns or hotels referred to are still in existence, and still open to the public; one or two lost inns are mentioned, that are too important to miss, but it will be obvious from the text which these are.

I should like to thank all those landlords and landladies who responded to my questions on the history of their establishment, and went out of their way to supply me with notes on their inn's history, or to point out features that survive there. Thanks are also due to my wife, Hazel, for accompanying me on so many forays around the countryside, for reading the proofs and for making numerous comments on the text.

Dane Love
Auchinleck, 1997

1   Inns Over the Years

Inns have played a very important part in Scottish life for centuries. An act of the Scottish Parliament passed in 1336, though it does not actually mention inns as such, refers to the beginnings of the trade. It states that 'All who sell bread and beer in burghs to receive travellers and supply their wants at the current prices; travellers who leave without paying to be arrested in the king's name'. A further act of 1366 stated that 'The chamberlains ordered to see that sufficient inns are provided in the burghs'. It was probably only the larger towns that supported inns at this period.

By 1424 the Scottish Parliament passed an act that promoted the establishment of inns throughout the country: 'In burghs and thoroughfares, hostelries to be provided with accommodation for man and horse'. Three years later a second act tried to ensure that this work continued: 'Inns to be established in all burghs for the reception of travellers and their horses'. These inns were not only created for the comfort of travellers, but were also a means of 'policing' visitors to the area. It was often felt that strangers to the district might be up to no good, and it was thought that a closer eye could be kept on them in public houses; an act stipulated that a traveller caught staying with friends when an inn was available nearby would be liable to a hefty fine of forty shillings Scots (about 17p).

The oldest real inns founded in Edinburgh are said to date

from the early fifteenth century. In 1498, when plague was
rife in the city, the council issued a statute ordaining that all
taverns and alehouses in the city should close at 10 o'clock in
the evening. This was supposed to help to prevent the
pestilence from spreading. Edinburgh inns were at this time
generally located below street level, in order that they be
'removed from profane eyes'.

At the end of the fifteenth century, and for much of the
sixteenth, the prices charged by innkeepers caused the
Parliament much concern. Various acts were passed that
determined suitable charges, such as the one of 1496, which
gave the right to 'Barons, magistrates and others having the
direction and rule of thoroughfare and hostelries to set prices
on victuals, bread, ale and other necessaries'. In 1535, 'For
eschewing exorbitant prices taken from travellers, the
statutes of James I and other sovereigns to be enforced; burgh
officers to cause hostellers to have sufficient accommodation
and food at the usual rate in the neighbourhood; the rate of
charges to be fixed yearly'. Sixteen years later the problem
was still there, so another act was passed, which stated: 'The
price of victual being doubled and trebled by hostellers, the
provost and bailies to fix the price for dinner and supper at
inns, so that the lieges be not grieved and hurt; a hosteller not
obeying the law to be deprived'. In 1567 it was decreed that
'The auld acts anent hostelries to be augmented and put in
execution'.

Innkeepers had a responsibility under the law that made
them quite important people in their communities. In
seaports, innkeepers were, by an Act of Parliament passed in
1493, obliged to 'answer to the king for the customs and
duties of strangers passing away uncustomed and for money
exported'.

Scotland does not have the same number of ancient inns as
England, because virtually every person brewed their own ale
and offered hospitality to travellers. Fynes Moryson, who
travelled in Scotland in 1598, noted that:

I did never see nor heare that they have any publike Innes with signs hanging out, but the better sort of citizens brew ale, their usuall drinke (which will distemper a stranger's bodie), and the same citizens will entertaine passengers upon acquaintance or entreaty.

After the Union of the Crowns in 1603, however, the English laws relating to public houses were copied in Scotland. Anyone wishing to sell ale or spirits had to obtain a licence. The first inns were licensed in 1604, and among those still surviving are the Kingshouse on Rannoch Moor, the Crook Inn in Tweedsmuir and the Spread Eagle Inn at Jedburgh.

For a long time inns had a reputation for being dens of iniquity. In Edinburgh in the sixteenth century there were so many inns run by landladies who basically ran brothels that the city council passed a law forbidding them to keep house. The law seems to have been quite ineffective, however, for in 1695 a new law was passed that decreed a fine of £3 Scots be paid by the owner or employer, should a woman be employed in an inn. At that time, and for many years afterwards, landladies in Scotland were known by the term 'Lucky', or 'The Lucky' (sometimes spelled 'Luckie'). In *Rob Roy*, Scott names the landlady of an old hostelry in Glasgow as 'Luckie Flyter', and in eighteenth-century Edinburgh, the landlady of the popular oyster cellar and bar mentioned in the poems of Robert Fergusson (1750–74), was Luckie Middlemass (or Middlemist).

The furnishings of an old inn were in general quite sparse. Apart from a series of unmatched but sturdy chairs, there may have been a sideboard or dresser, often with pewter or copper plates and bowls on display. There was invariably a large fireplace, round which the chairs were huddled. Drink was served in pewter flagons that contained one quart; these were known as 'tappit hens' from the handle on the lid, which was said to represent a crested hen. A number of inns had standard measures, and a few of these survive – the

Queensferry Museum has a half-pint pewter measure belonging to the Anchor Inn.

Games have been played in inns for centuries, but originally it was only smaller games, which could be played on a table-top. These included Nine Men's Morris, various card games, and dominoes. It was not until the early 1800s that games needing more space started to be introduced, among them skittles, bowls and billiards. However, with the growth of the temperance movement, such 'amusements' were seen as encouraging folk to frequent the inns, and they were gradually banned in many areas.

At one time, inns could be opened by virtually anyone. In 1756 the licensing laws were tightened up and extended, mainly for revenue purposes, but they only covered the sale of ale. Innkeepers had to apply to magistrates or Justices of the Peace for permission to keep an inn, but this was so easily obtained that the licences were little more than worthless pieces of paper. In 1780 Glasgow magistrates granted 605 licences, 94 of which were issued to persons unconnected with inns – masons, tobacconists, tailors, barbers and even rope-makers! In 1772 the same council proposed the removal of most of the city's hanging inn signs, for 'they interrupt the views along the streets, and darken the light of the lamps in the night-time'. Licenses that included spirits were not required until 1793, and it was not until 1828 that more restrictive and tightly controlled licensing was introduced. In that year the Home Drummond Act required the landlords of 'common inns, alehouses or victualling houses' to apply to the local licensing authority for a certificate to sell liquor. The magistrates of the Royal Burghs and the Justices of the Peace met twice yearly to consider applications for certificates, each of which had to be accompanied by a testimonial to the applicant's good moral standards, usually supplied by a minister or kirk elder. Inn-keepers had to comply with certain conditions laid down by the act, such as preventing 'men or women of notoriously bad fame' or 'dissolute girls and boys' from entering their premises, complying with weights and measures acts, and preventing certain unlawful games from taking place. Should a landlord be found guilty of failing to meet any of these conditions, he not only lost his licence, he was also liable to a fine or even imprisonment.

In Dumfries in the eighteenth century only burgesses were allowed to brew liquor, and then only if they had received a licence from the magistrates of the town for a small fee. The Dumfries bailies found drunkenness to be a problem at this time, and they introduced an act limiting the hours a tavern could remain open. Before receiving a licence, inn-keepers had to declare that 'no vitious or scandelous personnes shall be harboured or resett [received] in our houses, and that we nor any of our families sall be found drunk, and that we sall not sell drink to any persone or personnes within our houses on the Sabbath, and sell nor resett nor give drink to any personnes after nine o' clock at nyght; and that if we sall be at any tyme found contravenors of these presents, we sall pay for the first fault five merks, for the second ten merks, and for the third fault to be deprived of the libertie of brewing.'

The services available at inns varied widely from one to another. In some places the landlord would go out of his way to ensure that the visitor had everything he required, whereas in others the visitor was basically given little more than a roof over his head! It is recorded in many early accounts of tours through Scotland that the travellers carried their own cutlery, plates and cups with them. In his *Autobiography*, Dr Alexander Carlyle described some of the conditions as far as eating utensils went:

By this time [1742] even the second tavern in Haddington (where the presbytery dined, having quarrelled with the first) had knives and forks for their table. But ten or twelve years before that time, my father used to carry a shagreen case, with a knife and fork and spoon.... When I attended in 1742 and

1743 they [the inn] had still but one glass on the table, which went round with the bottle.

In 1829 the second Baron Teignmouth toured through the western islands, a journey which brought him to Armadale on Skye. He had hoped to stay with Lord Macdonald at Armadale Castle, but discovered that he was away from home.

It was necessary, therefore, to seek the Inn. A little girl trotted forward, and soon led me to a row of fishing-huts, imbedded in a hollow scooped out of the hill-side, one of which proved to be the Inn, containing two extremely small apartments: one the kitchen, without windows, its wall completely cased in soot, and apparently, as far as the eye could penetrate the dense atmosphere of smoke, crowded with inmates, whilst large quantities of fish and meat occupied the small interval between their heads and the ceiling, from which these stores depended. The other apartment was clean, and furnished with a bed; but as this was occupied by a young leddy, it was necessary that a bedding should be spread for me upon the floor. On my demurring to this arrangement, the young leddy disappeared, and the apartment was appropriated to the stranger. But never was a first ray of light more welcome than that which entered the single pane with which the chamber was furnished.

Better pleased with the service and conditions at the inns he visited was the Rev. John Lettice (1737–1832), an Englishman who toured Scotland as far north as Inverness in 1792. He noted that:

No country has handsomer or better inns than Scotland.... I have the highest commendation to bestow on the civility and attention of Scottish innkeepers.... Their houses everywhere but in the poorer districts of the Highlands are equal to our own in England: and the new ones established of late in most of the towns are undoubtedly superior in point of accommodation and elegance.

He stayed at the Tontine Hotel in Glasgow's Trongate, erected in 1783 but destroyed by fire in 1912. Like the Tontine in Peebles, which will be mentioned later, this was erected by subscription, its coffee room opening in 1784. Lettice described the magnificent apartment:

A grand bow, lighted by five lofty sashes, projects into the court of the hotel: all we could then perceive through them, was a space, apparently considerable, with a number of figures sitting, standing, or walking about. On entering, we found a room of seventy or eighty feet in length, with corresponding dimensions of height and breadth; having another vast window on one of its sides, mingling its auxiliary light with those of the bow. This was no other than the great subscription coffee-room; supported by certain annual contributions of more than six hundred of the principal citizens of Glasgow, and members of the university. Half the newspapers of London, the Gazettes from Ireland, Holland and France, and a number of provincial journals, and chronicles of Scotland and England, besides reviews, magazines, and other periodical publications, are objects of the Subscription. At the daily arrival of the post, a more stirring, lively, and anxious scene can hardly be imagined.

James Hogg travelled round the Highlands on a number of tours during the first decade of the nineteenth century. He stayed at numerous inns, some of which he mentions in his accounts of his travels. In 1802 he stopped at the Dalnacardoch Inn, which he found had graffiti on the walls of the rooms, cut into the plaster. He 'began to amuse myself by writing and, now and then, by reading notes on the plaister – with which the room abounded. And many of them were a little to the discredit of the inn.' The following year he stayed at the Dalmally Inn in Argyll, where he was able to eat a hearty breakfast, but he found the inn to have a poor appearance. 'Some of the windows [were] built up with turf, and, on pretence of scarcity of fuel, they refused to kindle a fire in my apartment, although I was very wet, and pleaded movingly for one.'

The standard of service at inns changed over time, much as it does today, with changes of proprietor or landlord. Writing in 1812, Elizabeth Grant of Rothiemurchus noted that:

The old inn at Blair [near Blair Atholl in Perthshire] was high up on the hill, overlooking the park, the wall of which was just opposite the windows. We used to watch through the trunks of the trees for the antlered heads of the herds of deer, and walk to a point from whence we could see the Castle far down below, beside the river, a large, plain, very ugly building now, that very likely looked grander before its battlements were levelled by order of the government after the rebellion. Here we were accustomed to a particularly good pudding, a regular soufflé that would have been no discredit to a first rate French cook, only that he would have been amazed at the quantity of whisky poured over it. The German brandy puddings must be of the same genus, improved, perhaps, by the burning, except to the taste of the highlander. The 'Athole lad' who waited on us was very awkward, red haired, freckled, in a faded, nearly thread bare tartan jacket. My father and mother had a bedroom, Johnny and the maid a closet, but we had three and our governess slept in the parlour, two in a bed, and the beds were in the wall shut in by panels, and very musty was the smell of them.... We never see such inns now; no carpets on the floors, no cushions on the chairs, no curtains to the windows. Of course polished tables, or even clean ones, were unknown. All the accessories of the dinner were wretched, but the dinner itself, I remember, was excellent; hotch potch salmon, fine mutton, grouse, scanty vegetables, bad bread but good wine.

The introduction of the Malt Tax in 1725 caused the price of malt to rise 3d per bushel. This resulted in an increase in the price of ale, which made it a less popular drink. It was at this time that whisky, which had previously been quite rare, became a viable alternative, and its consumption grew. No one was allowed to brew or sell liquor in many towns unless they were burgesses and had received a licence from the magistrates.

In the eighteenth and nineteenth centuries punch was a common drink. It was usually served cold, and the most common punch recipe contained Jamaica rum and water, in a ratio of one to two. To change the flavour to suit different tastes, lemon and lime juice could be added, or sugar and nutmeg. Most inns had their own large punch-bowls, and one of the few to survive is that from the Saracen's Head in Glasgow, now preserved in the city's People's Palace Museum.

Many inns originally brewed their own ale for sale, in brewhouses that were often located in cellars or at the rear of the premises, and the brews varied from establishment to establishment. Two main types of ale were made: 'Scotch ale' and 'tuppenny' (or 'small beer'). The former was a very strong and sweet beer, affordable only by the rich, and 'small beer' was a by-product of its manufacture. The latter, which tended to be weaker, was also known as 'tuppenny beer' – from its price per Scots pint (around two English quarts) at the time of the Union – and was the drink of the common man.

It was not until the foundation of larger brewing companies that brewing on the premises became uncommon, for it was then easier and cheaper to buy in beer from a manufacturer. The first such brewers set up in business in the late seventeenth century, but it was not until the early eighteenth century that the biggest firms were founded. In

Edinburgh Archibald Campbell commenced brewing in 1710, William Younger in 1749 and William MacEwen in 1856. Hugh and Robert Tennent set up in Glasgow in 1740, and George Younger began brewing at Alloa in 1762. The Belhaven Brewery at Dunbar, now the country's oldest brewery, was founded in 1719, and John Fowler brewed at Prestonpans from 1720. In the nineteenth century most large towns had breweries of their own, with the number of brewers reaching a peak of around 300, but as the twentieth century dawned a number were taken over or forced out of business by the larger companies. By 1960 the number had dropped to 27, falling further to seven in 1995. However, a number of small-scale breweries producing 'real ales' have now sprung up.

Porter became a popular drink in the second half of the nineteenth century. This bitter-tasting beer was in stark contrast to the sweeter Scotch ales that had been popular hitherto. Porter was at first imported from London, but soon Scots brewers were producing their own – among them the Anderston and Calton breweries in Glasgow. Porter was in due course superseded by pale ales and by lager, the new drink of the Edwardian period. Customers could drink imported lager from Germany, but Scottish imitations were soon being produced by Tennent's in Glasgow and Jeffrey's in Edinburgh.

Inns offered lodging to travellers and drink to thirsty folk, but many inn-keepers ran other businesses from them as well. Obvious trades were the hiring of coaches, the stabling of horses and the brewing of beer, but some inn-keepers ran less closely associated businesses. Many of the more remote inns had landlords who were also farmers. In 1814 James Hope, an agent for the Commissioners responsible for building new roads in the Highlands, noted that, 'No inn-keeper can exist without some farm at least'. Moreover, the sale of alcohol was not a monopoly of inn-keepers. At one time virtually anyone could offer drink on sale to the public, and it was often remarked upon by travellers from England that virtually every house in Scotland was willing to sell ale to anyone willing to purchase it. In 1814 William Ayton toured much of Scotland and kept a detailed journal. He writes of Annan in Dumfriesshire:

That whisky is the favourite drink of the people is very evident, not only from the prevalence of red noses, but from a direct notice that it is to be bought at every other house in the place. The vending of it is combined with every other trade, every dealer well knowing that, whatever may be his success in other ventures, he is sure of a few customers for this seductive cordial. Opposite to me, as I sat in the inn, I perceived a 'draper and dealer in spirits'; a little lower down is a 'grocer and dealer in spirits'; and in the town there is a still more extraordinary union, a 'banker and dealer in spirits'. Exclusive of these supplementary dealers, there are plenty of professed publicans, so that a stranger might suspect that this was the great whisky magazine of the nation, till he discovered that in the copiousness of its store it is only like every other town in Scotland.

Inns were the homes of numerous clubs that flourished around Scotland in the eighteenth and nineteenth centuries. Many were little more than a group of drinkers who met regularly in a particular tavern, whereas others were groups of learned men who met to pass on recent gleanings of research or information which would be useful to them in their careers.

Edinburgh had innumerable clubs, the list including the Cape Club, Friday Club, Gowks Club, Marrow Bone Club, Mirror Club, Oyster Club, Poker Club, Spendthrift Club and Sweating Club. In Glasgow clubs were just as popular. The City Club was a noted group of literary-minded individuals who met in the former Bank Tavern in the Trongate, and its members included Hugh MacDonald (1817–60), author of *Rambles Around Glasgow* (1854), and William Miller (1810–72), author of *Wee Willie Winkie*; it was later refounded as the Burns Club. The Garrick Club met in MacLaren's Inn in Dunlop Street; among its members were the artists Sam Bough (1822–78) and John Mossman (1817–90), and actor John Henry Alexander (1796–1851). The Anderston Club was a group of learned men who walked each Saturday from the city to the what was then country village of Anderston, to John Sharpe's Tavern. There they ate his celebrated howtowdie and mutton, and discussed the affairs of the city. The club was founded by the mathematician Dr Robert Simson (1687–1768), and Adam Smith (1723–90), author of the *Wealth of Nations*, was another member. Other Glasgow clubs included the Morning Club, which met at five in the morning at a tavern in Currie's Close, and the Grog Club, a group of ex-servicemen who met at the Black Boy Tavern in the Gallowgate. The Banditti Club was less respectable, for its members drank until midnight when they began roaming the streets performing practical jokes like upending sentry boxes and swapping shop signs around – what today would be termed vandalism. Their base was Gardner's Tavern in Gibson's Wynd. The oldest inn in Glasgow is said to be the Old Burnt Barns, which was established in 1679 at the corner of London Road and Ross Street; the name came from a great fire in 1668 which destroyed a number of grain stores in the vicinity. The present building is not the original, however, for it has been rebuilt in recent years, and is now known as the Old Barns.

The names and locations of the old inns in Edinburgh from the time of Queen Anne have long since been forgotten, but a number are referred to in the writings of Dr Pitcairn (1652–1713). This passage is from *To Strangers*:

At one time you may be delighted with the bowls of Steil of the Cross Keys; then other heroes, at the Ship, will shew you the huge cups which belonged to mighty bibbers of yore. Or you may seek out the sweet-spoken Katy at Buchanan's, or Tennant's commodious house, where scalloped oysters will be brought in with your wine. But Hay calls us, than whom no woman of milder disposition or better-stored cellar can be named in the whole town. Now, it will gratify you to make your way into the Avernian grottoes, and caves never seen of the sun; but remember to make friends with the dog which guards the threshold. Straightway Mistress Anne will bring the native liquor. Seek the innermost rooms and the snug seats: these know the sun, at least, when Anne enters. What souls joying in the Lethæan flood you may there see! what frolics, God-willing, you may partake of! Mindless of all that goes on in the outer world, joys not to be told to mortal do they there imbibe. But perhaps you may wish by and by to get back to the world – which is indeed no easy matter.

Dr Pitcairn is recorded as receiving visits from his patients at his seat in a tavern known to its regulars as the 'Greppa', located in a cellar off Parliament Close. There he would listen to their ailments and dispense advice to them.

Of the Edinburgh inns whose site is known, one of the most famous was Fortune's Tavern, located in Old Stamp Office Close, off the Royal Mile. The building had originally been the town house of the Earl of Eglinton. In the second half of the eighteenth century Fortune's was *the* place in Edinburgh, and it was here that the Lord High Commissioner of the General Assembly of the Church of Scotland stayed, and from here his cortège marched to the annual meeting. The inn was also home to the Poker Club, members of which included the notable: Hugh Blair (1718–1800), minister and professor of rhetoric and belles lettres; Adam Fergusson (1723–1816), philosopher and historian; David Hume (1711–76), philosopher and historian; and William Robertson (1721–1793), historian and king's historiographer.

John Dowie's inn stood in Liberton Wynd, between the

High Street and the Cowgate, and was a busy inn at the close
of the eighteenth century. It was later renamed Burns Tavern
– for Robert Burns is known to have frequented the inn, as
well as Robert Fergusson, David Hume, and Sir Henry
Raeburn – and later became a tourist attraction in its own
right, but it was demolished in 1834 to allow the
construction of the King George IV Bridge. Dowie's was also
noted for selling Younger's Edinburgh Ale, which has been
described as 'a potent fluid, which almost glued the lips of the
drinker together, and of which few, therefore, could despatch
more than a bottle'. This inn was noted for its lack of
daylight, being little more than a series of chambers, which, it
is said, decreased in size as one headed deeper into the inn,
with the last, small room known as the 'coffin', from its
diminutive size and dark appearance. John Dowie, who was
noted for his frugality, retired from the trade with the sum of
£6,000.

In Anchor Close stood Dawney Douglas' Anchor Tavern,
another hostelry frequented by Burns. This inn was the home
of the Crochallan Fencibles, a drinking club of which Burns
was a member. His poem 'Rattlin' Roarin' Willie' was based
on this notorious group, Willie being William Dunbar, a city
lawyer and 'colonel' of the Fencibles. The Anchor Tavern
was one of the better class of inns in the city, for it had two
principal doors, one of them leading to a superior room,
known as the Crown Room, which had two large windows
and was kept for special events.

In Writers' Court stood the Star and Garter, though it was
often better known as Cleriheugh's, after its landlord. In the
eighteenth century this inn was often frequented by the
magistrates and councillors of the city. It is mentioned in *Guy
Mannering*, where Scott wrote:

> Besides the miserable entrance, the house itself seemed paltry
> and half ruinous. The passage in which they stood had a
> window to the close, which admitted a little light during the

daytime, and a villanous compound of smells at all times but more especially towards evening. Corresponding to this window was a borrowed light on the other side of the passage, looking into the kitchen, which had no direct communication with the free air, but received in the daytime, at second-hand, such straggling and obscure light as found its way from the lane through the window opposite. At present, the interior of the kitchen was visible by its own huge fires – a sort of Pande-

Star and Garter Inn, Edinburgh

monium, where men and women, half undressed, were busied
in baking, broiling, roasting oysters, and preparing devils on
the gridiron; the mistress of the place, with her shoes
slip-shod, and her hair straggling like that of Megaera from
under a round-eared cap, toiling, scolding, receiving orders,
giving them, and obeying them all at once, seemed the
presiding enchantress of that gloomy and fiery region.

The use of the word 'hotel' to replace 'inn' became more
common in the second half of the eighteenth century. An inn
– which offered accommodation, in addition to selling
alcohol and providing refreshment, mainly for the use of
travellers – was seen as superior to a hostelry or public house.
Those inns which felt that they were even more superior
started to call themselves hotels, after the French *hôtel*.

A number of hotels were built in towns in order to boost
trade and commerce within the district. It was felt that a
better standard of inn would attract a better clientele to the
town for shopping and trade, and so various groups arranged
the construction of more elegant premises. The main builders
of hotels and inns were the local lairds, and often these hotels
had a secondary function; many were used to house those of
the laird's guests that he could not put up in his mansion. If
there was a large party at the house, only the top echelons of
society were given rooms there, the lower ones being
quartered in the laird's hotel. One example is the Seafield
Arms Hotel, which stands in Seafield Street at Cullen. This
was erected in 1822 by the Earl of Seafield, at a cost of
£3,000, and was originally known as the Cullen Hotel.
Classical in style, it had large stables adjoining and was one
of the finest hotels in the area; indeed the writer of the *New
Statistical Account* for the parish noted that it was 'the only
modern building deserving of notice'.

Other hotel builders were developers and businessmen. At
Kilmarnock the Merchant's Society built what was described
as 'a very elegant inn' at great expense in the early years of

the nineteenth century. The George Hotel was a major coaching inn, its immense size making it ideal for public meetings and even church services. The Burns Federation was founded here in 1885 (the town's Burns Club having met in the hotel since 1841). The large hall was later converted into a cinema, and the hotel closed in 1920, being converted into shops and offices.

The arrival of the railway in many towns killed off a number of old inns, for the railway companies often established their own 'Railway Hotel' or 'Station Hotel' next to the station. In large towns and cities these could be substantial buildings, and they killed at a stroke the trade of the coaching inns that had hitherto been the centres of community life. In Glasgow, the Glasgow and South Western Railway Company opened the St Enoch Station Hotel in 1880, complete with 200 bedrooms and a staff of eighty. In 1885 the Central Station Hotel was completed by the Caledonian Railway Company. The *Illustrated London News* described the building:

It is of vast size, as there are no fewer than 550 apartments within the building, giving accommodation for over 420 guests, in addition to 170 servants and officials.... In the carpeting of the establishment 1,000 yards of Axminster have been used for the staircase and corridors, 800 yards of Wilton for the public and sitting rooms, and 5,400 yards of Brussels for the bedrooms. From the various parts of the house 1,200 electric bells communicate with 600 indicators; the speaking tubes extend to fully 5,000 feet, weighing 4½ tons, and the wires in connection with the bells measure 29 miles and weigh 2½ tons.

Other large station hotels were erected in Aberdeen (1901), Ayr (1886), Inverness (1855). In Edinburgh the two main railway companies built one each, the North British Hotel (1895–1902), now the Balmoral Hotel, and the Caledonian

Hotel (1883), now the Old Waverley Hotel. And many towns and villages that are now a long way from the nearest railway – as a result of the Beeching cuts and other railway rationalizations – still boast a Railway or Station hotel. The Railway Tavern at Jedburgh, for example, is 34 miles from the nearest railway station.

Not station hotels as such, but closely connected with the railways, were hotels erected by the railway companies at tourist resorts. The Turnberry Hotel was opened in 1904, built by the Glasgow and South Western Railway Company and Marquess of Ailsa. Gleneagles Hotel at Auchterarder dates from 1924 and was built by the Caledonian Railway Company. Both these hotels are today better known for their association with the golf courses that surround them. The Cruden Bay Hotel in Aberdeenshire was built by the Great North of Scotland Railway in 1899 and had 140 rooms, electric lighting and a lift, as well as a golf course. The golf course survives, but the hotel was demolished in 1952. The Dornoch Hotel in Sutherland, built in 1902–4 by the Highland Railway Company still operates.

The erection of hotels at coastal resorts with the sole purpose of catering for the new phenomenon of tourists began towards the end of the eighteenth century. In the 1790s Nairn, which was noted for its fresh air, low rainfall, and bracing sea breezes, had an inn that had a bathing machine for hire. Purpose-built hotels followed, and many of them adopted names like Nairn's Marine Hotel (1860), later renamed the Royal Marine after Queen Victoria's grand-daughter Princess Maud and her husband, Prince Christian Frederick Charles George Waldemar Axel of Denmark – King Håkon VII.

Drunkenness became a problem in early nineteenth-century Scotland. In Edinburgh at that time pubs would open at six in the morning and stay open until eleven at night. In 1844 there were over five hundred places where one could purchase drink in the city, 53 of them in the Cowgate alone. The city fathers began to control the number of ale-houses – preventing new ones from opening and promoting the closure of inferior existing ones – and between 1834 and 1844 over a hundred places selling drink were closed in the capital.

Drink was fairly cheap, with whisky available at twopence per nip, or a half-crown a bottle, since the duty on whisky had been lowered in 1822 from seven shillings per bottle to two shillings and sixpence. As a result, whisky consumption increased almost threefold over the next seven years. Robert Louis Stevenson wrote, 'A Scot of poetic temperament, and without religious exaltation, drops as if by nature into the public house. The picture may not be pleasing; but what else is a man to do in this dog's weather?' Drink was on sale virtually everywhere, and the many ministers who contributed to the *New Statistical Account* of around 1840 complained of the number of inns and ale-houses. Typical of the hundreds of comments was the following of 1837 from Newton-on-Ayr in Ayrshire: 'There are thirty public houses or places where spirituous liquors are sold, which is in the proportion of one to every twenty-nine families – a number unnecessarily large.'

In Glasgow in the early 1800s there were reckoned to be public houses for every 130 folk, and it is said that every twelfth house in the city was a tavern of some type or other. From the Saltmarket up the High Street to the Cathedral, one visitor to the city counted no fewer than eighty places where he could have bought drink.

Sunday opening of inns had been frowned upon in Scotland for many years. In 1656 an Act of the Scottish Parliament decreed that inns should not be used on Sundays, unless one was a genuine traveller. (But even these often found that the meals available on the Sabbath were of an inferior quality. A *bona fide* traveller who arrived at a Hamilton inn on a Sunday in 1723 was offered nothing but bread, butter and perhaps an egg until after the evening service was finished, when a cooked meal was available.) William Forbes MacKenzie MP (1810–62) campaigned for the closure of public houses on a Sunday as a means of curbing drunkenness. This was approved by Parliament with the introduction of the Licensing (Scotland) Act of 1853, which also restricted week-day opening hours from 8 a.m. to 11 p.m. and forbade the sale of liquor within six miles of a toll-house. The Act also prevented the sale of alcohol in grocers' shops for consumption on the premises, and the sale of alcohol on Sundays in hotels, except to *bona fide* travellers. This last rule, however, was easily got round. Many people went for Sunday walks to their neighbouring town or village, where they could drink in the bars as genuine 'travellers' – invariably passing on the way people from that very neighbouring place, who were walking towards just those inns that they themselves were barred from! Another problem created by the Act was that of illicit drinking dens (or shebeens as they were known), which sprang up all over the country. Shopkeepers often sold drink illegally on a Sunday, devising secret signs to indicate whether they had alcohol on sale or not. At Lochgelly in Fife a shopkeeper was noted for his window display – if crossed pipes were shown he would be happy to supply you with liquor!

In 1903 an Act of Parliament set up licensing courts in burghs, with a population of over 4,000 people, and in counties. It also increased the penalties for those found in a drunken state.

In the nineteenth century total abstinence from alcohol became popular and was vehemently promoted by groups such as the Rechabites or Temperance Societies. John Dunlop (1789–1868), a lawyer from Greenock, and a noted philanthropist, is regarded as the pioneer of the temperance movement in Great Britain. In 1828 he visited France and was surprised to discover that Catholic France had higher morals where alcohol was concerned than Presbyterian

Scotland. He campaigned to focus attention on the facts, re-educate the public and thus break the extensive network of customs involving drink, but he found this difficult. However, temperance societies were founded in Maryhill and Greenock in October 1829, and within a year were joined by dozens more; from them grew the Glasgow and West of Scotland Temperance Society. William Collins, founder of the great Glasgow publishing and printing firm, soon joined Dunlop's movement, and from his presses there came hundreds of thousands of temperance leaflets. The Scottish Temperance League was founded in 1844, the Independent Lodge of Good Templars formed a Scottish Lodge in 1869, and in 1870 the Band of Hope Union was founded.

In Dundee a Scottish Prohibition Party was founded in 1901 to campaign for tighter drink laws. (In 1922 one of its leading members, Edwin Scrymgeour, successfully beat Winston Churchill at an election, and became Britain's only Prohibitionist member of parliament.) Campaigning went on at Westminster for many years, but a temperance act did not become law until August 1913, and, because of the Great War, was not implemented until 1919 (in the meantime the Defence of the Realm Act restricted the opening hours of public houses). The Temperance (Scotland) Act allowed residents to call for local elections to decide whether a community should become 'dry' or not. For an election to be called, one tenth of the electors had to request it, and 55% of the electorate had to vote for 'no licence' in order to make the area dry. A number of large burghs, such as Kilsyth, Kirkintilloch, Stromness and Wick became dry, as did a number of residential areas of Glasgow, including Cathcart, Kelvinside and Pollokshields. Later votes overturned these decisions in many areas, one of the last large towns to return to 'wetness' being Kirkintilloch, which voted for it in 1968, after being dry for 48 years. Veto Polls were abolished with the Licensing (Scotland) Act of 1976.

In Glasgow the council espoused the temperance

movement. In the late nineteenth century it had found itself the proprietor of over thirty public houses, acquired with slum properties that it proposed to demolish. A number of these inns were kept open for a time, but they were gradually closed as the buildings were replaced. It was then decided that new buildings erected by the council should not contain public houses, and none was erected on council property for years thereafter. This posed no problems in the city centre, but when new housing schemes were built at Castlemilk, Drumchapel and Easterhouse no public houses were included, and it was not until the 1960s that the council allowed public houses to be opened there.

In a number of areas it was realized that total abstinence was virtually impossible, and that it would be better to educate the people in temperate drinking habits. In the Lothian counties the Gothenburg System was adopted by many communities. This was based on a scheme which was popular in the Swedish city of that name. The Temperance Society of Gothenburg operated its own public houses, which were clean and closely regulated, and it used the profits to benefit the whole of society. In many inns, food or coffee was offered as an alternative to alcohol. (However, in 1895 critics of the scheme pointed out that there were four times the number of drunkards in Gothenburg than there were in Dundee – a city with a larger population!)

Armadale Public House Society was formed in 1797 and erected an inn at the Cross of this West Lothian town. This was not run on Gothenburg principles, but the Gothenburg name was revived when the society was reformed at a public meeting called in 1901 with the object of stemming the rising tide of drunkenness in the town. The meeting elected Malcolm Mallace as president, William Lowe as treasurer, and David Love and David Kerr as members of the management committee. Shares in the society were sold at five shillings each, but this failed to raise sufficient funds; undaunted, however, the committee approached a local coalmaster, who agreed to back the society to the tune of £1,000. Premises were rented in West Main Street, and the inn opened to the public. To boost the Society's profits, the prices charged were lower than those in any neighbouring hostelry. This guaranteed success; indeed, the inn's first year produced sufficient profit to pay the shareholders a 5% dividend, as well as raising the money to buy the premises it had been renting. In front of the inn an ornate arcaded clock tower was later erected as a memorial to Malcolm Mallace. Profits from Armadale Gothenburg were used to pay the wages of the barmen and cleaners (cleanliness was one of its main priorities), as well as to fund numerous community schemes. A district nurse was employed, an ambulance was purchased, a bowling green provided, as well as sponsorship for the local flower-show and band.

The Gothenburg Inn, Armadale

Other places that had Gothenburg inns included Cowdenbeath, where the Gothenburg House dated from 1895. The Black Bull in Dalkeith was built in 1905 as the Gothenburg Inn by the Dalkeith Public House Improvement Company. A modern building in the Arts and Crafts style, designed by Charles Greig, the inn had large windows and a restaurant at first-floor level; next door there was a (now demolished) block of houses also owned by the company and known as the Gothenburg Buildings. The Dean Tavern at Newtongrange still operates on the Gothenburg principle. It was built in the Main Street in 1910 by the local colliery company, and the profits were used to provide the village with a public park, as well as to introduce electricity to its houses. In nearby Gorebridge the Hunterfield Tavern, opened in 1911 on the same basis, was built by the Arniston Coal Company; its profits were also used to provide a park in 1930, as well as a cinema in the 1920s. In Glasgow, the Public House Trust Limited was founded in 1901, funded with 25,000 shares of £1 each. It was modelled on the successful Earl Grey's Public House Trust of Nottingham and, like it, tried to improve the conditions within public houses.

During the First World War two unique government controls over public houses were introduced in parts of Scotland – the only such schemes in the United Kingdom. In the Dingwall area, where a submarine base had been established, and around Gretna, where there were numerous munitions works, drunkenness was such a major problem that Lloyd George is known to have observed that, 'drunkenness amongst munitions workers is doing more damage to the war effort than all the German U-boats put together'. To counteract it a State Management Scheme was introduced which took control of the public houses in the two localities and regulated their hours; drunkenness and disorderly conduct dropped dramatically, and court appearances were sharply reduced. The scheme did not end with the war in 1918, but remained in operation at Gretna for 55 years.

Temperance Hotels grew in popularity in the nineteenth century, supplying bed and board to people who did not wish to stay in a building where alcohol was on sale. Hundreds were established all over the country, and many present-day inns or guest-houses owe their origin to them. Another type of hotel closely connected with the temperance movement was the hydropathic, or 'hydro'. Here the residents could improve their health, by breathing the fresh air and dipping in the cold waters of the pools. Turkish baths and cold-water showers were in vogue. At Moffat there were also mineral and vapour baths – in addition 300 bedrooms on five floors, a swimming pool, tennis courts and croquet lawns – and a guest at the beginning of the century was expected to pay £2 12s 6d per week, including food (with a supplement of seven shillings for August). Originally hydros banned tobacco and gambling, and were totally alcohol-free, but today they all contain bars – although Crieff Hydro did not have its bar installed until the early 1990s. Hydropathic establishments in Scotland include those at Crieff (1868), Dunblane (1875–8), Melrose (1869–71, now the Waverley Castle Hotel), Peebles (1878–80, rebuilt 1905 after a major fire), Pitlochry (1875), Portpatrick (1901–5), Rothesay (1843, now the Glenburn Hotel), and Seamill (1871). The hydros at Craiglockhart (1880), Deeside (now Tor-na-Dee Hospital), Forres (Cluny Hill Hydropathic Establishment, 1864), Moffat (1878, destroyed by fire 1921), Oban (unfinished, 1881), Shandon (1876, demolished) and Skelmorlie (1873, demolished) no longer function.

The principal development in hotel accommodation in the twentieth century has been the country house hotel. Hundreds of mansions became too large for their owners to maintain, and many were converted into luxury hotels. They have depended for their success on the advent of the private car and greater freedom of travel, for many country house hotels are a long way from towns or villages, but within travelling distance of the main scenic tourist attractions.

The Licensing (Scotland) Act, passed in 1976, allowed the return of Sunday opening and extended opening hours to 11 p.m. All-day licences and children's certificates were also introduced, and the whole ethos of public houses gradually changed. Bar meals were introduced in many areas for the first time and were soon regarded as a perfectly acceptable way of eating out. Families were welcome at Scottish inns, and the scourge of drunkenness was far less of a problem.

2   Coaching Halts

A large number of the old inns that survive in Scotland today owe their origin to the stage-coach, having been built in the eighteenth, or early nineteenth centuries, when travel by coach became more common. Before this the roads in the countryside were so badly rutted and so poorly looked after that it was almost impossible to travel along them for more than short distances, certainly in the winter months. In 1661 the Justices of the Peace were given powers to sentence criminals to statute labour on the roads, though this improved the roads but slightly. The first Turnpike Trust in Scotland was set up in 1714 in Midlothian, but things developed slowly. It was not until the Turnpike Act of 1751 became law that roadways improved all over the countryside, and between then and 1844 over 350 local Turnpike Acts were passed in Scotland. These acts allowed for the setting up of toll gates at various points along recognized routes, the fees raised going towards the maintenance of the roads.

During the 1780s John Loudon McAdam (1756–1836) invented and perfected a new method of building roads that was far superior to the methods hitherto used. His 'macadamising' process involved a base made of large stones, over which a layer of smaller stones was laid with a camber that allowed water to run off. The small stones were compressed by the action of wheels running over them, producing a fairly smooth road that gave a more comfortable ride. It was not until the mid-1890s that tar was added to bind the surface layer. Probably the first company to produce tar-macadam in Scotland was W.G. Walker and Co. of Ayr, which experimented with it in 1894 and was given contracts to surface some roads in Glasgow and other towns in 1895.

Probably the first public coach service had been set up in 1678 by William Hume, whose coach and six horses made the journey from Glasgow to Edinburgh and back in six days. This proved to be a financial failure, and the service was dropped. Improvements to the roads in the eighteenth century, however, meant that public stage-coach services could be introduced that were fairly reliable and likely to keep to their advertised schedules. In 1749 a new Glasgow-to-Edinburgh service was established, taking just two days between the cities, and in 1780 a newspaper advertisement for the 'Edinburgh to Glasgow Flyer' stated that the journey would take just over twenty-four hours.

A number of inns en route became staging posts where the coach-horses could be changed for fresh animals, which kept the speed up. To service the various competitors on the more northerly route between Edinburgh and Glasgow (which more or less corresponds to the modern A89) there were change-houses at Newbridge (where an inn of 1683 with a corbie-stepped gable survives), Broxburn (Buchan Arms, 1780), Uphall (Oatridge Hotel, formerly the Uphall Hotel, c. 1800), Bathgate (Bathgate Inn and Royal Hotel), Armadale (Star Hotel, late eighteenth-century), Blackridge (Craig Inn, c. 1790), the remote Forrestfield Inn, and thence through Airdrie and Coatbridge to Glasgow. Another important route went via the inns at Mid Calder (Torphichen Arms, c. 1763), Livingston Inn (eighteenth-century), Whitburn, Harthill, and Bellshill. By the end of the eighteenth century the improved roads meant that it took only six hours for a stage-coach to travel between Edinburgh and Glasgow.

Before such coaching inns were built, the taverns that travellers encountered on their journeys were like those that

Edward Burt described, in his *Letters from a Gentleman in the North of Scotland to his Friend in England* (1754), as 'mean hovels, with dirty rooms, dirty food, and dirty attendants'. He found the servants had no shoes or stockings, the tables had no covers and were thick with grease, and the butter was covered in cow-hairs. Meals were served without cutlery (one was expected to supply one's own!). The tariffs were cheap, however: Thomas Carlyle paid three shillings and sixpence for four days' board and lodging at an inn.

In 1831 a notable highway robbery took place on the Glasgow-to-Edinburgh route. When the stage-coach 'Prince George' left Glasgow one winter's day, the driver, Jock MacMillan, had only one passenger, who had paid to sit outside. This passenger had with him a large tin trunk, which he requested to be stored in the boot below the driver's seat, where it was chained and padlocked to the coach body. At Airdrie two men boarded the coach, paying to ride outside, and as it trundled on its way they spent the time cleaning an old, greasy chain, making quite a bit of noise. At Forrestfield, a man and a woman joined the coach and travelled as far as Armadale, giving Jock MacMillan a half-crown tip as they alighted. At the Royal Hotel in Bathgate the two men with the chain left the coach, leaving only Jock and the man with the trunk on board. At Uphall the coach arrived at the Oatridge Inn, where another man was awaiting it. He was to supervise the arrival of the trunk in Edinburgh, while the first man returned to Glasgow. When the two men, who were clerks of the Commercial Bank, went to check the trunk, they were shocked to discover that it had been forced and the £6,000 it contained stolen; a hole had been cut through the body of the coach to give access to it from inside the cabin. Investigations revealed that the stage-coach owner, George Gilchrist of Bathgate, was heavily in debt, and that only he knew that the bank would transport its money in this way. He was arrested, as was the 'woman' passenger, who turned out to be one George Davidson, clerk to the

Sheriff-substitute of Glasgow. (Davidson had forged a bond in the Sheriff's name, and he too was in desperate need of money.) At the High Court in Glasgow Gilchrist was sentenced to death, and he was hanged on 3 August 1831. Davidson was also sentenced to death, but his parents managed to help him escape from the gaol; he boarded a ship for Australia and later went to America, where he died a recluse in 1904.

A service between Edinburgh and London existed by the mid-eighteenth century, leaving from the Grassmarket and arriving in London around twelve to sixteen days later (a private chaise could have done the journey in only six days). The service was rather suspect, and the prospect of meeting highwaymen on the way was enough to persuade the more timid passengers to make out their wills before embarkation. A new coach service was introduced in 1754, and the *Edinburgh Evening Courant* of 1 July 1754 contained an advertisement describing it.

> The Edinburgh Stage-Coach, for the better accommodation of Passengers, will be altered to a new genteel two-end Glass Machine, hung on Steel Springs, exceeding light and easy, to go in ten days in summer and twelve in winter, to set out the first Tuesday in March, and continue it from Hosea Eastgate's, the *Coach and Horses*, in Dean Street, Soho, London, and from John Somerville's in the Canongate, Edinburgh, every other Tuesday, and meet at Burrow-bridge on Saturday night, and set out from thence on Monday morning, and get to London and Edinburgh on Friday. In the winter to set out from London and Edinburgh every other Monday morning, and to go to Burrow-bridge on Saturday night; and to set out from thence on Monday morning, and get to London and Edinburgh on Saturday night. Passengers to pay as usual. Performed, if God permits, by your dutiful servant, Hosea Eastgate. Care is taken of small parcels according to their value.

This service does not seem to have survived for very long, because in 1763 another new service began leaving monthly for London, with the frequency increased to daily departures in 1779.

In 1767 services were established from Edinburgh to Stirling and to Perth, one of the change-houses being the Star and Garter at Linlithgow, an old coaching inn in the main street. By 1825 there were more than fifty stage-coaches a day running from Edinburgh to various destinations.

The route currently taken by the A74 and M74, running up Annandale and down Clydesdale to link England with Glasgow, was first opened to coaching in the late eighteenth century. The Annandale road was rebuilt between 1777 and 1785, which allowed a two-horse carriage to run between Carlisle and Glasgow for the first time. The first run of the Royal Mail from London direct to Glasgow took place in 1788, averaging the 405 miles at 6 miles per hour. It reached the King's Arms Inn (now the Annandale Hotel) in Moffat on 7 July that year. A twenty-five minute break there allowed the horses to be changed and the passengers to be suitably refreshed – something that was in their interest, since they often had to walk up Ericstane Brae, the loaded coach being too heavy for the horses to pull!

Moffat became a major halt on the route north – apart from the Annandale there were posting establishments at the Buccleuch Arms (1760, replaced in 1863 with a larger building) and the Balmoral Hotel (1800) – but when Thomas Telford built a new, and less steep road up Evandale to the Beattock Summit (1814–19) the town was by-passed, and its coaching trade suffered. At the Evan Water bridge a new inn, originally known as the Beattock Inn, and later as Old Brig Inn, was erected in 1821–2 to Thomas Telford's plans by the Commissioners for Highland Roads and Bridges. It had stabling for fifty horses and over the archway into the yard was the legend 'Licensed to let Post Horses'. The inn has recently been converted into the Old Brig Rest Home.

In 1803 an Act of Parliament was passed which proposed the construction of roads and bridges in certain parts of the Highlands. One of the roads built as a result was the Great North Road between Inverness and Wick, and the branch from Bonar Bridge to Tongue by way of Lairg and the Crask and Altnaharra inns was completed in 1818. Many miles of these routes crossed land owned by the Dukes of Sutherland, and at Dunrobin Castle there is a collection of inn signs that gives an idea of how many inns were built on their estates around this time; all the signs bear the name *THE STAFFORD ARMS* (from the title of the heir to the Dukedom – the Marquess of Stafford) at the top, the inn's location at the bottom, and in between a coronet. Signs for inns at Port-Chamul, Traintell-beg (Trantlebeg), Eriboll, The Gaulan (Gualin), Bad-na-bea (Badnabay), Durine, Drum-hallastain, Achu-voldrach, Forse-an-aird (Forsinard), Bad-caul (Badcall) and The Moin (Moine) are displayed in the castle tea-room.

A report of 1828 by Joseph Mitchell, principal Road Inspector, comments on the Sutherland inns that:

> It deserves notice that, along all the Roads constructed by the Commissioners (extending in length upwards of 900 miles), suitable Inns affording accommodation superior to what could be expected, considering their recent introduction, have been erected or fitted up at regular stages; while formerly, even had other facilities existed, the total want of accommodation for Travellers would of itself present a serious obstacle to all internal intercourse.

And Thomas Telford's General Inspection Report of August 1828 noted that 'Along the coast of Sutherland there are commodious inns; at Golspie, near Dunrobin Castle, there is one equal to any to be found in England'. This, the Sutherland Arms, is a Z-shaped building distinguished by its ivy-grown walls. The centre block was erected in 1807–9 as part of the planned village scheme of Golspie, created by the Countess of Sutherland in 1805, and the north and south blocks, incorporating a coach-house, were added in 1826–7.

Contemporary with the construction of the road to Wick (the Great North Road) are a number of old inns in communities along its length. Near Dornoch, but on the main route north, stands the Trentham Hotel, a coaching inn named after the Duke of Sutherland's Staffordshire estate. Further north, at Helmsdale, the three-storey Bridge Hotel (or Inn), opened in 1816, stands at the end of Telford's 1811 bridge with a bay window facing the bridge; also in the village is the Belgrave Arms Hotel, built to plans by George Alexander in 1819. Helmsdale was at that time a three days' coach ride from Inverness. The coach route was extended from Wick to Thurso, where Caskey's Royal Hotel was a principal posting establishment (the present building was erected in Traill Street in 1864). The coach from Wick to Thurso was known locally as 'Sir John's coach' after Sir John Sinclair, whose campaign for the extension of the route finally succeeded when the new service was introduced in 1819. The coach averaged nine miles per hour over the twenty miles, and in the 1860s an outside seat to Wick cost six shillings; it continued to operate until 1874, when the railway arrived. West of Thurso, on the road to Tongue, the Strathy Inn was another important stop for coaches.

The Royal Mail was at first delivered in Scotland on foot by runners who journeyed between towns carrying letters. A runner operated from Dumbarton to Inveraray once weekly (around 1720), a distance of 47 miles, and in the summer of 1734 Archibald Campbell, inn-keeper at Inveraray and also postmaster in the village, recorded that over 2,450 letters passed through his hands (an average of 35 per week). In 1773 Samuel Johnson noted that the only real inn he found in the Inner Hebrides was at Sconser on Skye, which also doubled as the post office.

In 1784, when William Pitt the Younger was Prime Minister, the mail coach was introduced, carrying mail and passengers between the major cities. The first service to enter Scotland (1786) reached Edinburgh from London in sixty hours. In 1788 a second service between London and Glasgow was introduced. Mail from Glasgow to Edinburgh was carried by a post-boy on horseback until 1797, when it was announced that letters and parcels 'are now carried in a single horse-chaise by a person properly armed'. A service from Edinburgh to Aberdeen was introduced in 1798, after being delayed due to the poor condition of the roads. At the beginning of the eighteenth century there were thirty-four 'post-towns' in Scotland, rising to 164 by the end of the century, and by 1813 there were thirteen regular mail coach services in Scotland, covering the country from Portpatrick in the south to Inverness in the north, but mostly within the central belt.

The mail coach was the first-class method of travelling, quicker and safer than an ordinary chaise. It was quicker because the mail coaches did not have to pay tolls, and so were not held up at the toll-gates. The guard would blow his horn when the coach was about 250 yards away from the gate, and the toll-keeper was expected to have the gate open by the time it arrived. The mail coach was also regarded as a safer way of travelling, because there was an armed guard on board to look after the mail – a considerable deterrent to anyone contemplating highway robbery.

At first it was felt desirable that inn-keepers should also be the local postmasters, so that all services, from horse-changing to gathering letters, were under one roof. However, by 1784 opinions changed. Many inn-keepers were so busy with their primary occupation that they often delegated the post-office work to a servant, or even a chambermaid, and complaints were received that letters and parcels were sorted in bars and other public places. Post offices were thereafter usually operated by someone other than an inn-keeper, although in a few rural areas – where no one else had suitable premises or qualifications – some inn-keepers still operated the post office. A few hostelries continued to double as post offices until quite late. One was the Horse and Hound Inn at Bonchester Bridge in Roxburghshire; originally known as the Bridgend Inn, when it was erected in 1704, it was an important coaching halt on the route over Carter Bar into England. On 11 May 1835 the landlord's son, John Turnbull, was granted a licence to operate the post office (which he did from a small grocer's shop within the inn), and the post office remained at the Horse and Hound until 1907. The Atholl Arms at Dunkeld also contained a post office that was operated by the inn-keeper until 1927, when it was leased to the Postmaster-General for £72 per annum.

The stage-coaches had fairly strict timetables, and to meet these the horses were changed at either end of 'stages' of roughly eight to ten miles, which generally ended at inns. The number of horses kept at these inns was quite considerable, for some coaches required up to six horses to pull the six passengers who could afford inside seats, and the dozen more in cheaper outside seats exposed to the elements, as well as the coachman (and perhaps a guard) and all their luggage! As coach travel increased 'change-houses', or places where the coach-horses could be changed, were built, and these usually developed into inns, offering travellers food, ale and accommodation.

Many coaching inns were established by local landowners in order to boost industry and commerce on their estates. Often named after his family or titles, as we have seen, they were something of a status symbol, and thousands of 'Laird's Arms' inns were built in the eighteenth century – many of which survive as the older traditional Scots inn of today. Some of them remained in the ownership of the estate until fairly recent times – such as the Cambo Arms Inn near to St Andrews in Fife, which was built by the laird in 1780 and only sold in 1989. A few inns still belong to the local landowner, among them the Murray Arms at Gatehouse of Fleet in Kirkcudbrightshire or the Dalnashaugh Inn in Banffshire.

One of the main coaching routes into Scotland was along the road now known as the A7, stretching from Carlisle to Edinburgh. At regular intervals along it stage-houses were set up to cater for the travellers' and horses' requirements, and a good number still survive. The first village the road entered after crossing the border was Canonbie (now by-passed), where stands the Cross Keys Hotel, a seventeenth-century hostelry finished in the traditional black-and-white manner. At the next village on the route, Langholm, there are two coaching inns. The two-and-a-half-storey Eskdale Hotel was built in 1865 of dressed masonry and has rather distinctive arched windows. The original building of the Buck Hotel dates back to 1728, though it has been altered since. At the rear are former outbuildings which served as stables, a blacksmith's workshop and a small brewhouse (the inn made its own beer). Hugh MacDiarmid (1892–1978), who lived for a time in Langholm and whose monument stands on a local hillside, mentions 'the Buck and Croon hotels' in one of his poems.

The next stretch of the road is a long and arduous crossing of the border hills, with no real village or town for 22 miles until Hawick is reached. Just short of half-way – on the highest point of the road and on the border between Dumfriesshire and Roxburghshire – stands the Mosspaul Hotel. This old inn has welcomed weary travellers for many years, some of whom will be mentioned in more detail in Chapter 5.

Hawick has a fine selection of old hotels, though the Tower Hotel, its most noted coaching halt, has recently been converted into a visitor centre and museum. From here the road heads on another ten miles to Selkirk, with its three-storey County Hotel, and, after a five-mile drive alongside the Tweed, to Galashiels, the largest town in the Borders. Here the Kings Hotel in Market Street, a two-and-a-half-storey random-rubble building with sandstone dressings and Victorian gothic barge-boards, saw many coaches in its day.

The road to Edinburgh continues up the Gala Water to Stow, where the early nineteenth-century Manor Head Hotel catered for coaching traffic, before eventually dropping down from Fala Hill and Middleton Moor to North Middleton and the Middleton Inn: an old random-rubble building. Five miles further on the road drops into the valley of the South Esk at Lothianbridge, where there is a very traditional stone coaching inn, the Sun, the façade of which is adorned by five tiny gables and a small oval window. The building was erected in 1697 by James Chirnsyde. From here coach passengers had a pleasant ride of eight miles into Edinburgh, where many inns were established to cater for the trade.

Most of Edinburgh's old coaching inns have been lost over the years to redevelopment work in the city. The White Horse Inn, which stands in a close off the Royal Mile (31 Canongate), was one of the capital's most famous change-houses, though it has long-since closed and been converted into homes; it was from here the coaches for Newcastle and London departed. The inn's courtyard is still accessible through a pend (an archway running through the building), and is surrounded by former stables and outbuildings. According to Robert Chambers' *Traditions of Edinburgh*, this was the oldest house in Edinburgh 'to have been used in the character of an inn.' At the back of the alleyway – known today as White Horse Close, but for a time as Davidson's Close – stands the oldest part of the inn, with two external stairs. A datestone bears the inscription 16–3, with the third figure missing (it is thought that 1683 is the most likely date, although formerly the dates 1623 and 1523 have adorned the building). Access to the stables was from Calton Road to the rear of the inn, where eight arches stood, along with what was once a smithy.

Whitehorse Inn, Edinburgh

According to Chambers, 'the manner of procedure for a gentleman going to London in the days of the White Horse, was to come booted to this house with saddle-bags, and here engage and mount a suitable roadster, which was to serve all the way'. In Scott's *The Abbot*, Whitehorse Close is described as containing 'the inn or hostelry of St Michael, which stood in a large courtyard off the main street, close under the descent of the Calton Hill.... It was a busy scene, for the number of gentlemen and nobles who were now crowded into the city had filled all spare stables and places of public reception with their horses and military attendants'. In the same author's *Waverley*, the hero and Fergus MacIvor stay at the inn. Sir Walter also notes that on one occasion in 1737 a single letter was the sum total of mail being brought thither from London. The White Horse was also used for runaway marriages, and many young English couples came to Edinburgh to take advantage of Scottish laws that allowed them to wed without their parents' consent at an earlier age than was permissible in England. A pane of glass that used to be at the inn was inscribed with the names *Jeremiah and Sarah Bentham 1768*, who are thought to have been one of these couples. The White Horse Inn was partially rebuilt in 1889 as housing for workmen but degenerated into slums thereafter, until the Close was restored by Edinburgh City Council in 1965.

The White Horse Inn is often confused with James Boyd's Inn, 'at the sign of the White Horse'. This was located at the head of the Canongate, on the corner of St Mary's Street, and in the eighteenth century it had thirteen bedrooms and stabling for fifty horses. It was to Boyd's Inn that Dr Samuel Johnson went on his arrival in Edinburgh in 1773. (When Boswell met him there, he found the great lexicographer chastising the waiter for adding sugar to his lemonade without the use of tongs). At one time James Boyd, who was noted for his love of horse-racing, was facing ruin, but a white horse changed his luck; thereafter the symbol of the white horse was used as the inn's sign.

Three other major coaching routes led south from Edinburgh to the border before joining together at Newcastle upon Tyne. The first, which is now the A68, runs parallel with the A7 for a time before heading further eastward and crossing the border at Carter Bar. The first stop on the southward route was at Dalkeith, where the Cross Keys Hotel was erected around 1800 by the Duke of Buccleuch. This is a five-bayed building, with an archway through to where the stables used to be. Five miles further on is the Stair Arms at Ford, near Pathhead – an ancient corbie-stepped building with an old carriage preserved in its gardens. The visitor has less chance of seeing one of the Stair Arms' other presences: a chambermaid said to have been killed while working at the inn, for whose spirit makes only irregular appearances. A little further on the Fairshiels Inn, an eighteenth century coaching inn, stands at the foot of Soutra Hill, near Fala.

At Lauder is the two-and-a-half-storey Black Bull Hotel, finished in black and white and sporting a notable Venetian window. Alternatively, one could stop at the Eagle Hotel. This was originally a manse dating from the mid-seventeenth century, but in the early 1800s it was converted into a coaching inn, named after the eagles that formerly frequented the Lammermuir Hills. This inn is said to be haunted, but the ghostly spirit is rarely seen. At Earlston, eight miles further on, coaches might stop at the Red Lion Hotel in the square, before the five-mile journey to St Boswells. There, overlooking the village green, stands the red sandstone Buccleuch Arms Hotel, parts of which are said to date from the sixteenth century, though perhaps only the site. Nine miles on, at Jedburgh, the nineteenth-century Royal Hotel in the Canongate was ready to receive travellers, as was the Spread Eagle Hotel, standing in the High Street (another establishment laying claim to be Scotland's oldest hotel). From Jedburgh, a nine-mile ascent by the side of the Jed Water brought travellers to the border at Carter Bar, with the first inn in England five miles on at Byrness.

A second southward route branched off near Lauder and struck eastwards, passing through Greenlaw, where the classical Castle Inn Hotel probably dates from the 1830s. This road crossed the border at Coldstream, where the eighteenth-century Crown Hotel rises to three storeys in the Market Square, and the Newcastle Arms stands in the High Street.

Between the Carter Bar and Coldstream roads lies Kelso, an important market town. The classically styled Cross Keys Inn in the Square rises to four storeys, its central bay having a fifth storey. It was built by James Dickson MP of Ednam House in 1760 (although a smaller hotel is believed to have previously occupied the site) and claims to be Scotland's second oldest coaching inn. The inn boasted a ballroom and assembly rooms, and Robert Burns may have met his Caledonian Hunt patrons here, although he does not mention the inn by name in his diary (more definite visitors include Bonnie Prince Charlie and Beatrix Potter). It was rebuilt around 1880, when the present third storey and balustrades were added, replacing a Mansard roof.

In 1762 the Cross Keys was leased by John Waldie. In a contemporary newspaper he advertised:

This is to give notice that John Waldie of the Cross Keys Inn, in Kelso, has now procured 4-wheeled post-chaises and, as the road between Newcastle and Edinburgh by Kelso is now good and free of any interruption by reason of the bridge over the River Tweed at Kelso, all persons travelling that road will be supplied with good chaises, able horses and careful drivers at ninepence per mile, and travellers otherwise properly accommodated by their most obedient, humble servant, John Waldie.

An advertisement of 24 August 1833 details some of the prices and destinations available to the public from the Cross Keys:

The public are respectfully informed that the following Post Coaches continue to arrive at and depart from the Cross Keys Hotel, Kelso, as heretofore, at the following hours:-

Highflyer, betwixt London and Edinburgh – passes Kelso for the south, every lawful day, at half past eleven o'clock a.m. and for the north, at half-past three p.m.

Fares – From Kelso to London –	Inside	£3 10 0
	Outside	£2 7 0
From Kelso to Newcastle	Inside	£1 0 0
	Outside	£0 12 0

Tweed & Clydesdale Union Coach, betwixt Kelso and Glasgow every lawful day, by way of Melrose, Galashiels, Innerleithan [sic], Peebles, Biggar, Lanark, and Hamilton;

Cross Keys Hotel, Kelso

starts from Kelso and Glasgow every lawful morning at six o'clock.

Fares – From Kelso to Glasgow –   Inside   £1   4   0
                                  Outside   £0 12   0

This coach is driven through by one coachman – no Guard – arrives at Kelso and Glasgow each evening at seven o'clock. Border Union Coach, betwixt Kelso and Berwick, every lawful day; starts from the King's Arms Inn, Berwick, at eight o'clock in the morning and from Kelso at two o' clock afternoon, except on Friday's [sic], when it starts at half-past four afternoon.

Favourite, betwixt Kelso and Hawick, by way of Jedburgh, every Tuesday and Friday; starting from the Tower Inn, Hawick, at eight o'clock in the morning, and from Kelso at four o'clock in the afternoon, arriving at Hawick in sufficient time to meet the Heavy Coach from Edinburgh to Carlisle.

Passengers and Parcels for the above coaches booked at the Cross Keys Hotel, Kelso, where every attention is paid to the comfort and accommodation of travellers.

Another old coaching inn in Kelso is the Queen's Head Hotel in Bridge Street. This building was erected in 1725 when it was styled the King's Head, and rises to three storeys plus attic.

The third principal route to England from Edinburgh was that now taken by the A1 to the border at Berwick-upon-Tweed. At Haddington, sixteen miles from Edinburgh, horses could be changed at the George Hotel in the High Street, originally known as the Old Post House and later as the George and Dragon. This was originally built in 1674 and has a crenellated turret with Gothic lancet windows and is painted in the traditional black and white. A stable court, originally located at the back and entered through a pend, is now gardens. The George was one of the first post houses to be ready for business on the Great North Road, and the Yellow and Blue Mail, which operated between Edinburgh and London, changed horses here. Daniel Defoe, author of *Robinson Crusoe* and *A Tour Thro' the Whole Island of Great Britain* (1724–7), was a patron of the George, which he described as 'the best inn I have seen in Scotland, and inferior to none I have seen on the London Road'. Others who stayed there included Thomas and Jane Welsh Carlyle. In 1778 the Caledonian Hunt met here.

George Hotel, Haddington

In the next village, East Linton, there was a choice of hotels, between the Crown and Red Lion. If we by-pass Dunbar, the road leads to Cockburnspath, where the Cockburnspath Hotel is found, and then heads inland for a while, passing Grantshouse and Houndwood (near which is the Old Coaching Inn or Westwood House). Beyond Ayton is Burnmouth, some two miles from the border, where the cottage-like Flemington Inn, which has served travellers for centuries, advertises itself as the 'first and last in Scotland'.

Two of the coaching routes from Edinburgh towards England – those via Canonbie and Canter Bar – nearly meet at Melrose, which became an important centre for changing horses. There were a number of coaching hotels in this fairly small village, including the George and Abbotsford, the Bon Accord and the King's Arms, the latter a fine three-storey building which claims to be one of Scotland's oldest coaching inns.

The George and Abbotsford Hotel, formerly known as the George Inn, was built in 1740 on the site of the original High Church of Melrose, and at one time, when alterations were being made to the stables area of the inn, a cross of red sandstone cobbles was discovered, marking the site of the altar. At a later period part of the hotel's grounds was sold to provide a site for the building of a United Secession church – the landlord of the time, William Davidson, being an adherent. The George Inn was the third overnight stop south of Edinburgh on the coaching routes to Jedburgh or Newcastle. A former landlord, David Kyle, who was noted for his angling skills and was wont to take guests down to the Tweed and teach them how to fish, is mentioned by Sir Walter Scott in the introduction to *The Monastery*. Sir Walter stayed at the inn in 1803, meeting William and Dorothy Wordsworth there. This was before he built his mansion at Abbotsford in 1822–4, and the name Abbotsford does not appear to have been added to that of the George until around 1876.

The George and Abbotsford Hotel may be haunted although no one seems to have seen any apparitions. However, guests who stay overnight in rooms five to nine, which are on the first floor, often complain of hearing footsteps from the rooms above the ceiling – only there are no rooms above! Whether or not the sounds heard emanate from phantom soldiers is not known, but the hotel was used as a billet for Polish, and later American, soldiers during the Second World War.

To assist passengers alighting from coaches and horses, many inns had mounting blocks erected. These are small sets of stairs, three to five steps high, which made it easier to get into carriages or to mount horses. Few of these mounting blocks survive, but there is a very worn example outside the Auchinleck Arms in the village of the same name in Ayrshire (dating from around 1848, when it was known as the Railway Inn).

A good number of old coaching inns survive in south-west Scotland. The Queensberry Arms in Annan, one of the first towns reached after crossing the border at Gretna, was given this name in 1811, but it is known to have been in existence before then. In 1798 it was run by Edward Richards who had to pay tax on thirty windows. The hotel kept two post-chaises and ten livery horses, and to serve the travellers Richards employed seven servants who lived-in.

Thornhill, in Dumfriesshire, has two old inns in its wide main street. The oldest is the Buccleuch and Queensberry Arms, rising to two storeys, with attic rooms, and made of the warm, red Nithsdale sandstone. It was built in 1714 (at the same time as the rest of the village) as the Queensberry Arms, named after the laird, the third Duke of Queensberry, who lived at nearby Drumlanrig Castle; it was renamed sometime after the dukedoms of Queensberry and Buccleuch were merged in 1810. The George Inn was a later coaching hostelry built to serve the Glasgow to Carlisle mail-coach which was introduced in July 1788. Robert Burns is known to have visited each of these inns, both as a customer and in his official capacity as exciseman.

Castle Douglas, in Galloway, contains a number of former coaching inns, one of which, known as the King's Arms Hotel, is on a corner site in St Andrew Street. It stands two storeys in height and is finished in white rendering; it has been offering fare to weary travellers for over two hundred years. The archway through the building to the former stables survives, and the inn sign incorporates a stage-coach and horse. In King Street is the Imperial Hotel, with black-painted walls and another carriage pend through the centre of the building to the former stables. This coaching inn, which was used by excisemen and for posting, dates from 1820 and was originally known as the Globe Hotel. Preserved within it are some roasting jacks for cooking meat, which date from around 1790, and an urn with the hotel's name on it, as well as that of the nineteenth-century

Imperial Hotel, Castle Douglas

proprietor, Stephen Forbes. In 1920 the inn's licence was the subject of a major quarrel between the sitting tenant, Robert Gilchrist, and the new owner of the premises, Samuel Solley, who, having bought the building in which he had started his career as 'assistant boots', wished to run the hotel himself. The court granted the licence to Solley, on the condition that he run 'a thoroughly good hotel', and his descendants still own the business.

At Irvine, in Ayrshire, two old inns face each other across the High Street and must have been in competition for centuries. The King's Arms probably dates from the mid-eighteenth century and is a tall whitewashed inn, three storeys high. Many public meals were held here to celebrate various coronations and births of heirs to the throne, and before a Roman Catholic chapel was built in the town, masses were held here. Across the street stands the Eglinton Arms inn, three-and-a-half storeys high with faces carved on the pediments of its dormer windows. This was where at one time the teachers of the town's academy attended a dinner after the annual prize-giving, and where Irvine's first telephone was installed in the late 1880s.

At Kirkoswald, in the same county, is Kirkton Jean's Hotel, a coaching inn dating from 1792. Originally known as the Star Inn, it is known today as Kirkton Jean's after Jean Kennedy, who is mentioned in Burns' 'Tam o' Shanter'. Today the inn is made up of more than one building, the restaurant being located in what was Kirkton Jean's house. No ghosts have been seen in the inn, but there is a loft doorway in the restaurant which seems to move of its own accord, when no one is near it, something the present proprietors have observed a number of times.

At Ballantrae, in Ayrshire, the King's Arms Hotel dates from 1770 and, according to tradition, was built with stone taken from Ardstinchar Castle, whose ruins stand on the hillside above the village.

Before the Firth of Forth was bridged there was a ferry crossing at Queensferry, just west of Edinburgh. The coaching route from the northern landing to Perth went by way of Cowdenbeath, which was the first stopping place for changing horses. This was a tiny village, until coal-mining brought the sudden growth that earned it the title of the 'Chicago of Fife'. It was at its oldest hostelry, the Cowdenbeath Inn, that Queen Victoria's entourage stopped to change horses on her first trip to Scotland in 1842 – the only visit she ever made to Fife. Another coaching inn, the Commercial Hotel, was built in the late nineteenth century.

The second change-over place, and halfway halt, was the small former county town of Kinross, which still has a couple of interesting old inns. The Green Hotel (formerly Inn) so called because it was built on the site of the public green – was made ready for the first coach to pass through Kinross in 1787, when a service between Edinburgh and the Salutation Hotel in Perth, via the Queen's Ferry, was inaugurated. (The inn predates this time, however, for a traveller in 1772 noted that 'of these inns, none is more famous than Kinross Green Inn'.) The hotel's archives record the scene on the first day of the service in 1787:

> A post-chaise, painted in bright blue and festooned with flowers, drove through Inverkeithing and headed for Kinross. James Skelton, the owner of the Green Inn had decided to provide transport for travellers crossing the Queensferry Passage, and the sight of this object in the forecourt of the Green attracted custom and went a long way to putting the hotel on its feet.

The first mail coach, pulled by four horses, arrived at the Green Inn in 1799, and the increase in trade resulted in the inn being rebuilt in 1829.

Kinross became a major stopping point on the road north, and it is estimated that in 1849 twenty stagecoaches stopped there every day. A second inn in the town commenced a change-house service: the Kirklands Inn. Mrs Kirkland originally ran the Old Red Lion Inn (now part of the Victoria Bar) in Kinross – to which Robert Burns came, though he is said to have disliked his time there, due to a bout of colic. Mrs Kirkland had a new inn built which, in 1839, kept three post-chaises, a hearse, landau and 34 horses, and to service these she employed six strappers, four post-boys, an ostler, two waiters and four servants. For many years the Green and Kirklands inns competed for the passing trade. James Burns-Begg, a great grand-nephew of Robert Burns, recalls an incident from his youth when the servants and ostlers of the Kirklands Inn linked arms across the street to prevent coaches reaching the Green Inn, but the noted whip Sandy Miller forced his way through the line – and from that time onward his coach was renamed 'The Defiance'.

When the railway arrived at Kinross in 1858 mail was transferred to the trains, and the last coach, Mr Stalker's 'Lochleven Castle', gave up the service in 1859 (the Kirklands Inn had already laid off over sixty horses in 1848). The Green

Inn was abandoned for a number of years, becoming for a time a private house before being converted to a hotel, mainly for Loch Leven anglers, in 1879.

From Kinross coaches were driven over the Ochil Hills towards Perth. In Glen Farg, at the junction of three roads and three parishes, stands the Bein Inn, one of the oldest country inns hereabouts. Although quite old, the present building is not the original, and in *Between the Ochils and the Forth* (1888) David Beveridge describes the Bein Inn as a 'small but comfortable inn, much frequented by excursion parties from the Fair City. In the old coaching days this was the third and last stage on the road from Queensferry to Perth, but the building which then formed the inn is a little farther down the hill than the present caravanserai.' (When Queen Victoria did this journey she changed horses not at the Bein Inn, but further on at Bridge of Earn).

Fife did not have a service until 1812, when coaches went by way of North Queensferry, Kirkcaldy, Cupar and Woodhaven near Newport for Dundee and Aberdeen. In St Andrews, where the first coach arrived in 1829, two former coaching inns almost face each other in Market Street: the Cross Keys, built in 1851, and the Star Inn, which is of similar date. Near Methil, in the village of Windygates is the Windygates Hotel, which was built in the first half of the nineteenth century. Here one could change from the St Andrews-to-Queensferry coach to the coach bound for Pettycur and a different Edinburgh ferry. Windygates was by-passed by coaching traffic when a new route past Ladybank, Letham and Kilmany was promoted. On this route, a mile south of Freuchie at a major road junction, the New Inn was opened to cater for the travellers; this inn is often listed on Fife's milestones.

The 'city' of Dunkeld (its church was once a cathedral) is still a popular resting place on the great route north. In the street known as the Bridgehead stands the Atholl Arms Hotel (originally the Duke of Atholl's Arms Inn), built around 1790 as a coaching inn. According to Black's *Picturesque Tourist*, published in 1882:

Atholl Arms Inn, Dunkeld

Her Majesty the Queen [Victoria], in her journal of her life in the Highlands, has been graciously pleased to take note of this hotel as being very clean and having such a charming view from the windows. The Empress of the French, with her son, the Prince Imperial, also visited this hotel, and was pleased to express her entire approval of all the arrangements. Every attention is paid to the comfort of all visitors.

The hotel has a framed certificate which confirms that Victoria 'stopt' here in 1844, on her way to Blair Atholl, and partook of 'Scottish fare'. She probably did not experience the hotel's ghost – 'Chrissie', a parlourmaid who died at the hotel – whom some say they have seen roaming the corridors at night. Another old coaching inn in the town is the Royal Dunkeld Hotel, built in 1809, the same year that Telford constructed the bridge over the Tay.

The five-in-hand coach service from Glasgow to Fort William began in 1843, with its first section operated by a steamer travelling the length of Loch Lomond. This coach route was only operated from the middle of June to the middle of October, due both to the lack of custom and to unpredictable weather in the winter months. From Ardlui, at the head of the loch, the route used old inns, already established for the use of drovers, at Inverarnan, Crianlarich, Tyndrum, Bridge of Orchy, Inveroran, Kingshouse, Clachaig, Ballachulish and Corran, many of which will be mentioned elsewhere in this book.

Near Garve, north-west of Inverness is the Altguish Inn, remotely located in Strath Garve, near Loch Glascarnoch. This inn was on the Ullapool for the Western Isles coach route and was established as a coaching stop. Like many others, it advertises itself as 'one of Scotland's oldest inns'.

Coaching inns continued to be the focus of much of village and town life for over a century, but the arrival of the railway killed them off. Steam trains did not require rests or changes of horses every half dozen miles or so, and their speed was phenomenal compared with that of the stage-coach. The main railways in Scotland date from the nineteenth century, and by the time they reached their zenith in the early twentieth century virtually every large town or village had at least one station, and hundreds more served country houses, hamlets, shooting lodges and piers. Only inns close to railway terminals were able to enjoy the greater traffic which a railway could bring, and these were the ones that prospered. New 'Station Hotels' were built in many towns to cater for railway passengers and these were often in a different part of the town from the older establishments.

The coaching inn struggled to survive. Its vacant stables were often left empty, or let out to small businesses. Many were converted into billiard and smoking rooms, like the stables through the pend of the City Arms Hotel in Dunfermline, converted in 1909. Some were left to rot for a while until, as tourism became important, they were converted into additional bedrooms. With the advent of the motor car, many hotel stables were adapted as garages, either for parking guests' cars overnight, or else to provide petrol, servicing and bodywork repairs – as in the case of the Dumfries Arms in Cumnock, where the former stables, across the main street, are now the Central Garage. At Kilbirnie former inn stables were converted into a museum of local history, but in many cases – in particular in towns and cities, where space is at a premium – coaching stables were demolished and redeveloped.

3   Sailors' and Smugglers' Howffs

Hundreds of inns were established at ports, harbours and other coastal locations, to serve alcohol to seamen and provide accommodation for travellers. This chapter will look at a number of the different reasons why inns were established by the sea and also at inns associated with smuggling, be it coastal or whisky-related.

A ferry terminus was one common place for an inn. Ferries used to be far more common than they are today, and many crossings of quite narrow stretches of sea, or of rivers, had to be made by boat. If a traveller arrived at a ferry when the boat was in mid-crossing, or at night, then he had to wait for the next boat, and inns were opened to cater for the needs of such people. In many cases the inn was run by the ferryman himself, or the ferry-house sold whisky and offered accommodation.

There are dozens of hotels and public houses which still have names like 'The Old Ferry Inn', or 'Ferryhouse Hotel', and many more owe their origin to being located at a ferry point. The Airds Hotel at Port Appin was formerly known as the Old Ferry Inn, or at least, the older part of it, comprising the dining room and rooms above; the inn dates back to around 1700. It was at Port Appin that the 30-ton steamship *Comet* arrived in December 1820. She was the first

ocean-going steamboat, built at Greenock in 1812 by Henry
Bell of Helensburgh, and for the previous eighteen months
had been transporting passengers from Glasgow, through the
Crinan Canal and along the west coast to Fort William,
taking two days in each direction. She had just left Port
Appin in a snowstorm on 15 December when she was
wrecked on Craignish Point. The hull was split in two, the
stern swept towards the Gulf of Corryvreckan. All the
passengers managed to scramble ashore.

The Kylesku Bridge in Sutherland replaces a ferry which
formerly plied across Loch a' Chairn Bhain. On the south
side of the loch stands the Kylesku Hotel which used to be a
very popular place for taking refreshment while awaiting the
return of the ferry. The inn was originally known as the
Ferryhouse and dates from the eighteenth century, though it
has been rebuilt and extended many times over the last two
centuries. A tale tells of a local fisherman who found a barrel
of whisky on the nearby shore, probably flotsam from a ship
that had sunk in the Minch. He dragged it back to the
Ferryhouse and put it in an upstairs attic, which was
accessible by way of an external stair, and invited a number
of friends to the inn to share his good fortune. As the night
wore on the party became more riotous, and his son tried to
stop the festivities (for it was almost the Sabbath), but this
only made things worse, and a fight broke out in which the
son knocked his father down the stairs and broke his neck.
In severe agony, just before he expired, the father placed a
curse on his son. Within a short time the boy was on a fishing
trip in the sea-loch when he fell overboard and was drowned,
his corpse being washed up later on the shore of Loch
Glencoul. It is said that the ghost of the father still haunts the
oldest part of the Ferryhouse of Kylesku, reappearing on the
anniversary of his death.

On the island of South Uist stands the Lochboisdale Hotel,
at the port of the same name. The hotel was erected in 1882
at the same time as the new pier was constructed, in order to

benefit from the increase in trade that it brought. Another hostelry on the island, the Pollachar Inn, at its southernmost tip, is said to have been a haunt of smugglers, being remote and ideally placed for a quick crossing to the neighbouring islands of Eriskay and Barra. It was on the island of Eriskay that the *Politician* ran aground in 1941, carrying a large consignment of whisky; the ensuing 'liberation' of the thousands of bottles was the basis of Sir Compton Mackenzie's novel *Whisky Galore*.

At the end of the eighteenth, and throughout the nineteenth century, fishing was promoted as an industry in the north-west of Scotland. The British Fisheries Society was founded in London in 1786 to promote sea fishing and to establish new ports in the Highlands where the catches could be landed; its first governor was the fifth Duke of Argyll. The society established new settlements at Ullapool, Tobermory, Pulteneytown at Wick, and Lochbay on Skye, the last-named being a less successful venture than the others. As well as creating some form of harbour or pier, homes for the fishermen and stores for their nets, it also established an inn in each community, both for the use of the residents and for the benefit of travellers.

The inns at Tobermory and Ullapool were first promoted in 1788, when an advertisement in the *Aberdeen Journal* sought people to build in each community 'an Inn, consisting of a parlour, and proper offices, and cellars below; and of two storeys, exclusive of that for garrets above. – The walls must be of stone, the roof of slate.' The inn at Ullapool was designed by Robert Mylne and erected within a short time; it cost £800 to build and was described by a contemporary as 'too good for the probable resort to that place'. Furniture worth £113 3s 4d was transported to the inn from London, but many of the bedsteads were found to be too large for the rooms in which they were to be placed! The British Fisheries Society agent and his wife were appointed the first inn-keepers. The inn proved to be comfortable and as a result successful, and in 1793 an extension was built to contain a public bar. This inn served fishermen and tourists to Ullapool for many years, but was gradually by-passed for other hotels which were larger and more modern. It was rebuilt in 1973 and named the Arch Inn, from the archway through the building.

The inn at Tobermory was erected at the head of the bay, next to the mouth of the March Burn of Mishnish. Building began in 1790 and an inn similar to that at Ullapool was erected. There had previously been a 'Change House and brewhouse' here. At Lochbay, on the north-west corner of Skye, the new fishing community failed to expand like the others. Here, on the headland of Waternish, overlooking the bay, a row of houses named Macleod Terrace was built, one of which was the inn. Whether or not this row incorporated the original Stein Inn of 1648 is not known, but the present inn (which was 'modified' between 1790 and 1800 by Thomas Telford) claims to be the oldest on Skye.

There are a few inland inns which have connections with boats: those sailing on the adjacent canals. One of the better known is the Union Inn at Falkirk, at the junction of the Forth and Clyde Canal with the Union Canal, next to Lock 16. The three-storey building, which stands at the foot of the old locks that enabled boats to descend from the Union Canal to the lower level of the Forth and Clyde Canal, dates from around 1790 and is a fine Georgian structure built by the canal owners to serve refreshments to travellers. Another well-known hostelry on the Union Canal is the Bridge Inn at Ratho, west of Edinburgh. A two-storey building with a white front and black-painted quoins, the inn was built around the same time as the canal, when it was known as the New Inn. In 1973 the proprietor launched a barge, *Pride of the Union*, on the canal, which doubles as a floating restaurant; the Bridge Inn is now the hub of the Edinburgh Canal Centre.

Many coastal villages have old inns that are associated with smuggling. The illicit importation of liquor, salt, tea and East

Bridge Inn, Ratho

Indian goods was such a temptation to many landlords that they often provided the land-based side of this trade. Many other goods were also smuggled, however, from hair powder, paper and oranges, to linen, combs and mirrors. In fact, if the duty on an item was such that it could be brought in from abroad and sold illegally below the legal price, then there was a temptation to do so. After the Union of 1707, when Scottish taxes were brought into line with those of England, many nationalists felt that depriving the London government of the duty was perfectly respectable. In 1736 the 'Smuggler's Act' was passed, which introduced the death penalty for a smuggler convicted of assaulting or using arms against a Revenue Officer. Duties payable on various commodities around 1800 were as follows:

Brandy	22s 6d	per gallon
Calicoes and muslins	7d	per square yard
Candles	3d	per pound
Linens and cottons	3½d	per square yard
Rum	13s 1½d	per gallon
Salt	15s	per bushel
Silks (printed)	1d	per square yard
Spirits – Scottish	6s 2d	per gallon
– English	10s 2¼d	per gallon
Tea	96%	of value
Tobacco	3s 2d	per pound
Wine – French	11s 5d	per gallon
– other	9s 7d	per gallon

The Galloway coast was a popular location for smuggling, because of its proximity to Ireland and the Isle of Man. At Auchencairn, near Dalbeattie, is the Old Smugglers Inn, a white-washed traditional hostelry. The many inlets and tidal bays on the shores hereabouts made this an ideal countryside for hiding rowing-boats and stores of brandy, rum, lace, tobacco and wines, and Heston Isle was a popular landing place. The Smugglers Inn is home to a ghost known to the locals as 'Old Gladys'. She has made an appearance a number of times, and on other occasions when her spirit is not seen, she is known to be there, as objects seem to move around without anything touching them; on one occasion, during a dinner party at the inn, a powder compact rose out of a handbag which was sitting on the floor. Gladys is upset when anyone sits on what she regards as her seat by the fireside, and usually manages to convey her displeasure to that person. On one occasion, while Border Television was filming at the inn, a very faint figure appeared on the film which no one had noticed as the cameras were rolling.

Near Auchencairn is the Balcary Bay Hotel. Originally a country house built in 1625, it was bought twenty years later by three partners, Messrs. Clark, Crain and Quirk (the last is said to have been the head of a 'county family'), who were proprietors of what they termed a 'shipping company', though this was just a front for their smuggling trade. They brought goods from the Isle of Man and stored them in the hotel's cellars (now a bar) where the walls are five feet thick and the doors open seawards. Balcary House, as it was known, was raided in December 1777 by Inspector General Reid of H.M. Customs and Excise; the house was later sold to the proprietors of the Ayrshire and Galloway Railway Company as being suitable as a terminus hotel with adjoining port. On a cliff half a mile south of the hotel, overlooking the Irish Sea, is a hollow in the rock called Adam's Chair. This is supposed to be named after a free-trader who sat here to watch for his boats coming in towards Auchencairn Bay and signal to them whether it was safe to land or not.

At Isle of Whithorn is the Steam Packet Inn, named after the Isle of Man steam packet which used to sail from the little harbour there. The inn, which overlooks the harbour, has a painting of the steamer *Countess of Galloway* over the entrance doorway. Further west, nearer Stranraer, the little Cock Inn, – scarcely more than a roadside cottage – sits at the head of Auchenmalg Bay with its gable facing the sea. Smugglers used to row in to the beach here, and the inn is but a stone's throw from the shore. Although the smuggling side of the inn's business was illegal, it is said that the Cock Inn holds the oldest licence in Wigtownshire.

From the coast a number of upland tracks and paths went by way of remote inns towards Edinburgh. At Kirkcowan was a noted Smugglers Inn. From here the goods were taken further inland towards the House of the Hill Inn, and thence east through the Galloway Highlands towards Moniaive and Penpont. It was at the latter village that Robert Burns (who was appointed an exciseman in 1789, earning £32 3s 7d per annum) came into close contact with some smugglers. At one of the inns in Penpont he suffered an assault at their hands and called for help from a passer-by; a man who refused to help was later charged.

Smuggling was just as popular on the east coast. South Queensferry on the Firth of Forth was noted for its smugglers, many of whom frequented the Stag's Head Inn and the Queensferry Arms. It is said that the Black Castle in the High Street was their headquarters, and that a secret tunnel led from here to the shore (as with all secret tunnels, however, its location is now lost). The Smugglers' Inn at Anstruther in Fife dates from the late sixteenth century but was extended in the nineteenth century (there had been a previous inn on the site, which was said to date back to 1300). White-painted with black window-surrounds, it sits beside the Dreel Burn, over-looking the harbour. In the late seventeenth century the owner was Henrie Smyth, burgess and bailie in Anstruther Easter, who refused to renounce the Solemn League and Covenant in 1662. The inn was originally, and officially, a coaching inn. However, smuggling was rife along this coast, and the traders in illegal imports brought their contraband to the Isle of May before bringing it to the mainland on small boats via the Dreel Burn and the Smugglers' Inn. A number of secret underground passages are said to connect the inn with various neighbouring houses, but their location is no longer known. The inn is also said to have some form of spirit haunting it, but appearances are extremely rare.

Two old Fife inns have connections with one of the major incidents involving smugglers. The inn in Anstruther's High Street (which no longer exists) was known variously as James Wilson's Tavern, or the Smugglers' Howff, and was a favourite haunt of the free-traders. Andrew Wilson, one of

Smugglers' Inn, Anstruther

Fife's most notable smugglers in the first half of the eighteenth century, was originally a baker in the village of Pathhead, near Dysart, but found smuggling to be more lucrative. One night in January 1736 a considerable load of brandy was brought ashore at a place known as Wullie Gray's Dyke, between Cellardyke and Caiplie. The brandy was taken to a store in Cellardyke from where it was moved, once more under the cover of darkness, to the Smuggler's Howff. Not long after the transportation was completed, customs officers made an entry, confiscated all the contraband and, as was the custom, auctioned it off.

Andrew Wilson was left with few possessions, and so planned to rob the excisemen on one of their trips. He travelled to Edinburgh where he spoke to two friends (one named George Robertson, the other surnamed Hall) who were willing to take part. They crossed the Firth of Forth by ferry to Kinghorn, where they hired horses from Patrick Galloway, and set out for Anstruther. On reaching James

Wilson's Inn Wilson and his friends found out that excisemen – James Stark, the Collector, William Geddes and Alexander Clark – had left and were heading back towards Kirkcaldy, so they turned back in pursuit. They caught up with the excisemen, at Widow Fowler's Inn (now demolished) in Pittenweem's Marygate, where they were lodged for the night, and forced their way up towards the bedroom. The excisemen were so scared that they jumped out of the window in their night-clothes and ran away; Stark and Geddes hid, frightened for their lives, but Clark had the sense and strength to run barefoot back to Anstruther where he alerted the military. Wilson and his accomplices meanwhile took the £200 that they had left behind.

The three men were arrested fairly quickly and taken to jail at the Tolbooth in Edinburgh. The day before their execution they were taken to the Tolbooth Church, and during the service Wilson grappled with the warders and yelled out to Robertson to 'Rin, Geordie, Rin'. Robertson made his escape and was never found by the authorities again. Wilson's actions elicited sympathy from the populace, and he became something of a public hero; nevertheless, he was hanged in the Grassmarket.

The crowd who had turned up to witness the execution became restless, and the unpopular Captain John Porteous of the City Guard ordered his men to shoot; as a result about eight men were killed and many others injured. Porteous was tried and found guilty of wilful murder and placed in the Tolbooth. However, a delay in the execution resulted in a second riot, in the course of which the Tolbooth was forced and the captain taken by a mob towards the Grassmarket where he was hanged from a dyer's pole on 8 September 1736. In the following days two hundred or more residents were questioned about the incident, but the two who were tried in court were found not guilty.

The site of Widow Fowler's Inn in Pittenweem is marked by a shield-shaped plaque which reads:

Near this spot stood the inn where the Tax Gatherer was robbed by smugglers giving rise to the Porteous Riots 1736. Sir Walter Scott has immortalised the event in *The Heart of Midlothian*.

On the north shore of the Firth of Forth, south of Dunfermline, is the Ship Inn at Limekilns. A two-storey, four-bayed building, it stands to the west of the harbour, overlooking the firth, and is said to have been visited regularly by press gangs in the course of their business. In Robert Louis Stevenson's *Kidnapped*, written in 1886, David Balfour and Alan Breck begged food and passage across the Forth here.

In Limekilns we entered a small change-house, which we only knew to be a public by the wand over the door, and bought some bread and cheese from a good-looking lass that was the servant.

The excisemen were not only interested in illicit spirits brought into the country from abroad; they also spent much of their time chasing those who distilled illegal malts on the moors of the Highlands. Many an illicit still produced a palatable whisky, which was sold at a far cheaper price than official whiskies on which the duty had been paid. Excise officers spent much of their time trying to trace these stills, or else the whisky which had been produced in them.

The Freeburn Inn (or Hotel) near Tomatin, dates back to the 1820s, having been built to replace an older inn at Dalmagarry in Strathdearn, just over a mile nearer Inverness; it gets its name from the Allt na Frithe which joins the River Findhorn at the hotel. One day two officers of the excise (known as gaugers because they had to 'gauge' how much alcohol was in the whisky and thus determine how much duty was due) who were transporting a confiscated barrel of illicit whisky to Inverness stopped at the Freeburn Inn for the night, because of failing light. They lay down to rest in an upper room, with the barrel safely placed on the floor between them. However, the person from whom the barrel had been confiscated had followed the excisemen. He arranged for the inn's maid to enter the men's room on some excuse and, whilst there, to count how many floorboards there were from the wall to where the barrel lay. In the room below, the still-keeper counted a similar number and drilled a hole through the floorboards and into the barrel. Throughout the night the whisky slowly drained into a second barrel in the room below; next morning, the gaugers discovered to their surprise that the barrel was now empty, and that there was now no evidence for the prosecution.

A similar tale is told of the Bogroy Inn, which stands beside the main road near Kirkhill, but another incident involving illicit distilling is also associated with the Bogroy Inn. An excise officer investigating a report of a still somewhere in the upper reaches of Strath Glass was severely injured in a fight when he came across the hidden still. He managed to make his way the ten miles or so to the inn, where he was put up for the night, but by the next day he had died of his injuries.

The Corrymuckloch Inn near Amulree in Perthshire is today a farm, but it used to be a popular drover's inn on the old military road. A fight took place here between a number of whisky-smugglers and the gauger, who had the protection of a group of Scots Greys. The smugglers were the winners in this instance, and a popular poem of the time describes how the gauger was dealt with:

> But Donald and his men stuck fast –
> An' garr'd the beardies quit the field;
> The gauger he was thump'd gie weel,
> Afore his pride would let him yield.
> Then Donald's men, they a' cried out,
> 'Ye nasty, filthy, gauger loon,
> If ye come back, ye'll ne'er win hame,
> To see yer Ouchterarder toon.'

In Strath Avon is the clachan of Ballindalloch, erected at the gates of the castle of the same name. Here, where there is a magnificent by-passed bridge across the River Avon, stands the old Dalnashaugh Inn, still owned by the MacPherson-Grants of Ballindalloch. For many years the inn attracted drovers as they made their way across country, but it also has a connection with the illicit whisky industry. A tale survives of a group of gaugers, heading towards the whisky lands of Glenlivet on a wild and stormy night, who called in at the Dalnashaugh to break their journey. The landlady, guessing that they were excisemen, offered to take their sodden boots to dry by the fire; as she approached the fire, she dropped them into a pot of boiling water 'by accident'. The boots shrank, and by the time the excisemen had managed to stretch and dry them again, word had reached the distillers whose pots and stills miraculously disappeared!

A mile or so west of Kinlochard, in Stirlingshire, is a cottage known as Teapot. Originally this was the Teapot Inn, but drink is no longer served here. It is said that the inn got its name from the time when whisky was distilled illicitly in the hills hereabouts. Visitors to the inn would ask for a pot of tea, and if the landlord knew them, their teapot would be served with whisky inside it. If the landlord did not know the visitor, or was in any way suspicious, then what was served was a pot of boiling tea!

A notable late case of an illicit still came to court on 8 January 1934. The proprietor of the Gordon Arms Hotel in the inland town of Keith received a visit from the police, who were investigating another matter. They asked to inspect the hotel's cellars, which the proprietor showed them, but he claimed that a locked 'cupboard' did not have a key, and that he had never been in it. The police sensed that the hotelier was a bit nervous, and, perhaps suspecting stolen goods or some such thing, made a forced entry. Inside they found a whisky still and associated equipment. Among the items seized were a 'copper still, with a capacity of twelve gallons, a copper worm, 15.7 proof gallons of spirit fairly good, indeed quite good quality; thirty-six gallons of wash; a liquid in preparation of being made into spirits; three or four gallons of low wines and feints; eighteen packets of yeast; three bushels of malting barley, and a considerable quantity of vessels and utensils for use with the still'. The hotelier had built a flue from the cellar into a hole in the main fireplace which prevented the smoke from being noticed. At the Sheriff Court in Banff he was charged with 'between September and 29 December 1933, in an underground cellar at the Gordon Arms Hotel, without being licensed to do so, had or used a still for distilling and rectifying spirits, brewed or made wort or wash, and distilled low wines, feints and spirits in contravention of the Spirits Act, 1880, thereby being liable to a fine of £500 and forfeiture of all materials and utensils'. A haulier from the town was also charged with aiding and abetting. The Sheriff found the accused guilty, and fined the hotelier £150 and the haulier, who had distributed the hooch in Aberdeen and other places, £50.

A good many coastal villages and towns have old hotels or inns bearing the name 'Ship'. At Irvine the much-restored Ship Inn was built of whinstone from Dundonald as an ostlery and stables in 1597. In 1754 it was rebuilt and licensed as an inn to serve the sailors from the adjoining harbour, (which makes it the oldest pub in Irvine), after coming into the ownership of Charles Hamilton, Collector of Customs for Irvine port and town councillor, who had a monopoly for the sale of alcohol at the harbour for many years.

In Eyemouth, the Ship Hotel, a fine double-storey building with a Flemish-style gable also overlooks the harbour. In the 1700s an ale-house and rum-shop operated here, and it gradually expanded to take in travellers; no doubt it played host to smugglers also, for which the area around Eyemouth was notorious.

The Old Ship Hotel on Leith's Shore is a multi-gabled building, its façade dating from the mid-nineteenth century. The inn dates back to the sixteenth century, however, and part of the present building is said to date from the seventeenth century. A New Ship Inn, dating from the seventeenth century, used to stand beside it, but this has been demolished, save for its heavily moulded stone door jambs. The Old Ship Hotel has a carving of an ancient sailing ship in bold relief on the wall. The poets Robert Burns and Robert Fergusson both frequented the Old Ship, and both are known to have spoken kindly of the good cheer and food available. In 1822 King George IV came to Scotland – the first monarch to do so since the Jacobite uprisings – and landed on Scottish soil for the first time at Leith, where a plaque marks the spot; the Old Ship commemorated this visit with a stained-glass window dedicated to the king, and for many years after the event the hotel amplified its name to the Old Ship Hotel and King's Landing. Other old Ship Inns can be found at Stonehaven (dating from 1711), Banff (late eighteenth century) and Kirkwall in Orkney (seventeenth century).

At Newhaven, in what is now part of Edinburgh, one can find the Peacock Inn, or Hotel, at one time also known as Ye Olde Peacock Hotel. Its first owner was Thomas Peacock, a vintner, who petitioned the city of Edinburgh in 1767 for permission to convert some old cottages into a hostelry where he began serving mouth-watering fish teas, a simple but satisfying meal of haddock, chips, bread and butter and a pot of tea. The business was continued by a Mrs Clark who erected the present building; she also served 'Real and Original Clark's Newhaven Fish Dinners'. Many notables went to the Peacock to sample its famous fish teas – in the nineteenth century the list including Sheriff Alison, John Blackwood, William and Robert Chambers, Charles Dickens, Henry Irving, Douglas Jerrold, Charles Kean, Lord Robertson, Alexander Russel, and William Makepeace Thackeray. Dickens is recorded as having said, 'This is immense! The service is not so fine as it is at Greenwich, but the fish! and the cooking!' The writer, Charles Read (1814–84) stayed at the Peacock Inn whilst researching his novel of life as a fisherman, *Christie Johnstone*.

At Catterline in Kincardineshire the Creel Inn is associated with the artist Joan Eardley (1921–63), who stayed there on holiday before deciding to settle in the village. She painted many coastal and village scenes hereabouts, and one of her paintings hangs in the inn. In the cliff-side village of Gardenstown, east of Banff, stands the Garden Arms Hotel, erected in 1752 and named after the local lairds, the Gardens of Troup. Gardenstown, or 'Gamrie' as the locals prefer to call it, and as the parish is officially titled, is a strongly religious community, with many residents being members of the Exclusive or Open Brethren or other religious groups. This underlay a most unusual court case in February 1954, in which two men were accused of committing a breach of the peace by swearing in the Garden Arms. They were said to have used words such as 'bloody' and 'damn'. The proprietor of the hotel, Norman Tennant, stated that, 'It was blasphemous language, uncommon in a village like Gardenstown, a very respectable village'. The charge was 'Not Proven', a fine old Scottish verdict which implies that there was not sufficient evidence to convict the defendants, but too much to state that they were not guilty.

A few miles westward along the coast is the village of Portsoy, with its old harbour surrounded by attractive stone buildings. One of these used to be the Star Inn, dating from 1727, but in the 1960s it was converted into houses by Portsoy Town Council. The inn was popular with sailors from the harbour, which it overlooks. It is said that during the Napoleonic Wars this was a popular smugglers' howff, and there is another tale that a sea captain was murdered there. Today the scene is more peaceful, the building retaining its attractive pend and the remains of its cobbled courtyard. Further west again, the village of Findhorn, once the principal port of Morayshire, has a couple of interesting old sailors' inns. The present village dates from 1701, its predecessor having been engulfed by the sea and destroyed (in fact, there had also been a yet earlier village in existence, which was also washed away in major storms). The Crown and Anchor Inn dates from 1739, a study harled building with corbie-stepped gables. The nearby Kimberley Inn is newer, dating from 1777 and has an outside stairway on the front.

In the High Street of the attractive coastal village of Crail, in Fife, stands the Golf Hotel which the proprietors claim to be one of the oldest licensed inns in Scotland. At the entrance there are three steps down from the roadway – a sure sign of antiquity, for it is claimed that roads rise from three to four inches every century. According to local tradition, there has been an inn on this site since the early fourteenth century, but the present building is not so old and probably dates from the early 1700s – perhaps from 1721, the date on a marriage lintel over the fireplace in the public bar which bears the initials of Thomas Young and Isabella Martin. Two other interesting old stones are also incorporated in this wall. One, a coat of arms, was originally a dormer pediment from Cambo House (now demolished) and bears the initials of Thomas Myreton and his wife, Catherine Lindsay, daughter of the fifth Lord Lindsay. Sir David and Sir Thomas Erskine of Cambo owned the inn in the mid-1800s. The other stone is the base of a sun dial, perhaps also from Cambo House. The bar has an old ceiling with beams, one of which is circular in section (it is said that when a beam had to be replaced the local joiner used an old ship's mast).

Externally the Golf Hotel is also interesting. As well as being finished in the traditional black-and-white paintwork of so many Scots inns, it also has an attractive gable in the centre of the façade and one corner which is chamfered. This was to allow the roadway to squeeze past. Corbels above the chamfer allow the roof to be kept square. Part of the inn is built over a stream, which still flows beneath the old stables; most of it has

Golf Hotel, Crail

since been covered over to create a yard.

On the 23 February 1786 the Crail Golfing Society, now the seventh oldest club in Scotland, was founded in the hotel. One of the founder-members was the landlord of the hotel, Daniel Conolly, and the inn was used as the clubhouse for many years thereafter. It was probably sometime after this that the inn was renamed the Golf, for it is thought to have been known as the Thane of Fife in earlier times.

4   Drovers' Stances

Driving 'black cattle' from the Highlands south to the markets of London became one of the major industries of Scotland from the Union of Parliaments in 1707 until the nineteenth century, when the advent of the Highland railways killed it off. (Black cattle were not necessarily black in colour; they were usually dark red, and similar to what we now call Highland cattle.) The highland glens provide plenty of grazing during the summer months, but as winter approaches the grass becomes scarcer and the snows set in. As a result the cattle were normally sent to market in the autumn. The cattle, and latterly sheep, were gathered from numerous crofts across the countryside and driven south by way of drove roads towards market stances. Better known as 'trysts', these took place at Crieff from the early seventeenth century until around 1770, when they were moved to the Falkirk area and took place successively at Polmont, Roughcastle and then Stenhousemuir until, by the turn of the twentieth century, the markets had ceased. Along the drove roads – which were not always roads as we think of them, but more 'routes' through the open countryside – inns sprang up to cater for the thirsts and accommodation requirements of the drovers; at many there were common grazings or 'drove stances' (indeed in many cases the stances would have predated the inns). Almost every inn of any antiquity alongside these routes can lay claim to be a 'droving inn', for hundreds were erected to serve the passing trade. The network of drove roads covered virtually the whole of the Highlands, and those who wish to find out more about them can do no better than consult Dr Haldane's classic work, *The Drove Roads of Scotland*, first published in 1952 but reprinted a number of times since.

At a number of recognized places the cattle had to be swum across stretches of water, and inns were often established at either end of such passages, to give cattle and drovers a chance to dry off before setting out again. The narrowest stretch of water between the Isle of Skye and the mainland is the Kyle Rhea, five hundred yards wide, and it is reckoned that in the 1820s some 7,000 cattle crossed this stretch each year, forced to swim by being tied by a rope to a man in a boat. On the mainland at Glenelg stood an old inn that was visited by Johnson and Boswell. Johnson wrote:

> we were told that at Glenelg, on the sea-side, we should come to a house of lime and slate and glass. This image of magnificence raised our expectation. At last we came to our inn weary and peevish and began to inquire for meat and beds.
>
> Of the provisions the negative catalogue was very copious. Here was no meat, no milk, no bread, no eggs, no wine. We did not express much satisfaction. Here however we were to stay. Whisky we might have, and I believe at last they caught a fowl and killed it. We had some bread, and with that we prepared ourselves to be contented, when we had a very eminent proof of Highland hospitality. Along some miles of the way, in the evening, a gentleman's servant had kept us company on foot with very little notice on our part. He left us near Glenelg, and we thought on him no more till he came to us again, in about two hours, with a present from his master of rum and sugar. The man had mentioned his company, and the gentleman, whose name, I think, is Gordon, well knowing the penury of the place, had this attention to two men, whose

names perhaps he had not heard, by whom his kindness was not likely to be ever repaid, and who could be recommended to him only by their necessities.

We were now to examine our lodging. Out of one of the beds, on which we were to repose, started up, at our entrance, a man as black as a Cyclops from the forge.... Sleep, however, was necessary. Our Highlanders had at last found some hay, with which the inn could not supply them. I directed them to bring a bundle into the room, and slept upon it in my riding coat. Mr Boswell being more delicate, laid himself sheets with hay over and under him, and lay in linen like a gentleman.

Boswell described the same night:

We came to the inn at Glenelg. There was no provender for our horses; so they were sent to grass, with a man to watch them. A maid shewed us up stairs into a room damp and dirty, with bare walls, a variety of bad smells, a coarse black greasy fir table, and forms of the same kind; and out of a wretched bed started a fellow from his sleep, like Edgar in *King Lear*, 'Poor Tom's a cold'.

This inn was furnished with not a single article that we could either eat or drink; but Mr Murchison, factor to the Laird of Macleod in Glenelg, sent us a bottle of rum and some sugar, with a polite message, to acquaint us, that he was very sorry that he did not hear of us till we had passed his house, otherwise he should have insisted on our sleeping there that night; and that, if he were not obliged to set out for Inverness early next morning, he would have waited on us.

John Spencer-Stanhope arrived at the Glenelg Inn in 1806 and found the conditions even worse than those experienced by Boswell and Johnson:

There was nothing at all to eat, beds there were none, there was not even a chair! There was indeed a room which they offered *either to us or to our horses!* Wet, cold, weary and

hungry as we were, we determined, in preference, to face the
storm and cross over to Skye. We therefore left our servants to
take care of the horses and persuaded some boatmen by the
bribe of a large sum to take us over.

The present inn at Glenelg, created out of old coaching mews,
is much more attractive!

It was not only salt-water crossings that had to be made.
Loch Awe in Argyll – narrow, but twenty miles long – was
one of the barriers that had to be swum. Cattle brought up
Glen Nant from Taynuilt arrived at the lochside at North
Port (where stands the Taychreggan Inn, a notable drovers'
haunt) and were swum five hundred yards across to
Portsonachan (where the Portsonachan Hotel is also an old
drovers' inn) before being driven on to Inveraray.
Portsonachan means the, 'port of peace', and it remains a
quiet place today. The ferry rights between here and North
Port were originally granted to the Portsonachan innkeeper
as early as the fifteenth century, on condition that he ferried
the chief of the Campbells (later the Duke of Argyll) and his
retainers free of charge. Portsonachan later became an
important halt for the loch steamers that were popular at one
time.

Another important swimming point for cattle was across
Loch Long – a sea loch – between Rubha nan Eoin, a
headland beyond Carrick Castle, and Portincaple. At the top
of the ridge above Portincaple is the clachan of Whistlefield,
which has an old drovers' hostelry, with many ruinous pens
and stables around it. When the military road from Inveraray
and Dumbarton was completed in 1768 this swimming point
was abandoned, and the inn lost a lot of its custom.

A number of drovers brought their herds down through
Cowal towards either Ardentinny or Dunoon, further down
Loch Long, from where they were ferried across to Coulport
and Gourock respectively. The Ardentinny Hotel, dating
from 1720 or thereabouts, a two-storey building painted

white with black dressings around the windows, was formerly an old droving inn. There are some, however, who claim that bits of the present hotel are at least four centuries old, for Mary Queen of Scots is said to have rested here on her way towards Inveraray with her half-brother, the Regent Moray, in 1563 (the present Earl of Moray is a frequent guest at the hotel). Sir Harry Lauder, the famous Scots entertainer, used to be a regular; he lived for a number of years at Glenbranter House nearby, and one of the bars is named in his honour. The Ardentinny Hotel is also said to be haunted by small children who appear irregularly in one of the bedrooms.

Kilmelford, south of Oban, was one point where cattle shipped from the islands of Seil and Luing were landed and driven along Loch Avich to Loch Awe. The Cuilfail Hotel here was originally a drovers' inn, and part of the building dates from the droving period, though what is seen today is largely of the Victorian era. The poet John Keats stayed here in 1818.

The drove routes from Glencoe and Kinlochleven crossed the west end of Rannoch Moor and descended to Forest Lodge and Loch Tulla, at the head of which stands the Inveroran Inn, another old drover's rest. This inn actually replaces an older one, which was built straddling the road (some say that, because of this, it may once have been a toll-cottage). This older inn was the home of Mairi Bhàn Òg – daughter of the innkeeper, Nicol MacIntyre – who was courted by and married Donnchadh Bàn MacIntyre (1724–1812, better known as Duncan Bàn, poet and song-writer), who was born at Druimliaghart, half a mile or so to the west. In 1844 the Earl of Breadalbane tried to close the drovers' stance at Inveroran, for he felt it was disturbing his deer forest. The drovers, under the leadership of one MacGregor, fought this, taking their case to the Court of Session and claiming that the stance was vital to their trade. The drovers won their case, but Lord Breadalbane appealed to the House of Lords, which overturned the verdict, and the stance was closed in 1846. A new stance was created at Tyndrum, nine miles further south.

James Hogg and the Wordsworths stayed at Inveroran. Dorothy Wordsworth described the scene in her journal:

> About seven or eight travellers, probably drovers, with as many dogs, were sitting in a complete circle round a large peat fire in the middle of the floor, each with a mess of porridge, in a wooden vessel, upon his knee; a pot, suspended from one of the black beams, was boiling on the fire; two or three women pursuing their household business on the outside of the circle, children playing on the floor. There was nothing uncomfortable in this confusion: happy, busy, or vacant faces, all looked pleasant; and even the smoky air, being a sort of natural indoor atmosphere of Scotland, served only to give a softening, I may say harmony, to the whole.

The meal provided was not great, 'the butter not eatable, the barley-cakes fusty, the oat-bread so hard I could not chew it, and there were only four eggs in the house, which they had boiled as hard as stones'. When Robert Southey and Thomas Telford passed by the inn in 1819, the former described it as a 'wretched hovel' but was pleased to note that Lord Breadalbane was in the process of having a new building erected (probably the present one). This inn became a noted sporting hostelry, and climbers made it their base in the early days of the Scottish Mountaineering Club (founded 1889).

Drovers often walked their cattle something like nine miles a day, and from Rannoch Moor southwards old inns appear at fairly regular intervals. At Tyndrum was an inn that was formerly maintained by Lord Breadalbane, to whom this countryside at one time belonged, and a smithy where the cattle could be shod – for here the open moors were left behind for the enclosed roadways south. The village was a busy place when the drovers passed through. In 1799 Sarah

Murray of Kensington stayed here at the time that the drovers were returning north from Falkirk. As the night began to fall the number of men arriving at the inn grew. 'This continued till the house was in a perfect uproar: my servants could not get a place to put their heads in. My man took his sleep in the carriage: and the poor horses were almost crushed to death in the stables.' The inn at Tyndrum no longer survives, its place occupied by later hotels.

In Glen Falloch, above the head of Loch Lomond, there is another ancient drovers' hostelry. The Inverarnan Inn is a substantial stone building of two-and-a-half storeys, dating from 1705. It later became a popular stopping point on the grand tour round Scotland, and many writers have referred to it. Nathaniel Hawthorne, who stayed in 1857, experienced his first 'Scotch mist' here, when the 'clouds came down and enveloped us in a drizzle, or rather a shower, of such minute drops that they had not weight enough to fall'. In the late nineteenth century the inn also became a favourite haunt of the more well-to-do climbers, many Glaswegian outdoor folk making it their base for mountain sojourns. In his classic work, *Undiscovered Scotland*, the late W.H. Murray tells how he and two friends broke into the inn during appalling weather in the January of 1939. It was half past five in the morning, and they suspected Glencoe to be blocked by snow. After taking an ice-axe to a window to get in, the three slept until midday in what they reckoned must have been the bridal suite, since the bed was big enough for three!

Fifteen miles south, on the west side of Loch Lomond, the Inverbeg Inn is another drovers' resting place. It has been considerably extended over the years, but the oldest part dates from 1814. Cattle were driven down to Balloch at the bottom of the loch before proceeding eastwards, by way of Killearn, to the tryst at Falkirk. Some went via the village of Fintry, where the Clachan Hotel, which dates back to the seventeenth century, was also a drovers' halt.

Another route from Glen Falloch to Falkirk struck

south-east to Glengyle and ran down Loch Katrine and on to
Aberfoyle. Nine miles east of Aberfoyle is Thornhill, where
the Lion and Unicorn (which used to be known as the
Commercial Hotel, but changed its name around 1953)
claims to be a drovers' inn dating from 1635. Inside is a huge
fireplace, and tales of the ghost named Annie. She is a shy
person, dresses in green and is regarded as a 'kind and happy
ghost'; Elizabeth Taylor, who stayed at the Lion and Unicorn
in 1980, did not see her! An earlier visitor to the inn was Rob
Roy MacGregor, and in earlier centuries the inn seems to
have been frequented by cattle thieves and rustlers, who, if
necessary, could make a quick escape across the Moss of
Flanders (since drained).

In the centre of the Isle of Skye is the Sligachan Inn, in a
remote spot where the road from the south forks for Portree
and Dunvegan. Today it is a popular resort for climbers and
fishermen, but it owes its origin to the drovers, for this was
the stance for a regular cattle market. It later became an
important coaching stop on routes to and from the mainland.
In 1835 Alexander Smith spent *A Summer in Skye* and
recorded his experiences in book form. Of the Sligachan he
noted that his old guidebook gave it a poor write up, but he
found it,

> a perfect palace, when contrasted with the cart in which I
> have been soaked and shaken. In fact it is a recent building,
> infinitely superior to the old one. Its situation is the dreariest
> spot that could have been selected for the abode of man: it
> stands at the base of the mountains, just in front of a torrent
> which, for a hundred yards on each side of its channel, has
> strewn the ground with fragments of rock, hurried down from
> the crags. Such is the view from my bedroom, which serves me
> for parlour also. The interior however is more cheerful, and I
> am enjoying extremely the humble luxury of a peat fire, while
> the clean napkin on the table and the fine coloured tea-things,
> invite me to a sober meal.

Joseph Mitchell arrived at Sligachan two years later and attended the cattle market. In his *Reminiscences of My Life in the Highlands* he described the scene:

> The south country drovers attend and purchase from the breeders and farmers.... The debts that are contracted at other periods of the year are here generally discharged, and there is thus a most heterogeneous collection of people – tacksmen, farmers, drovers, cottars, factors, shopkeepers, innkeepers, many women, and gillies great and small. There are, besides, the extensive droves of cattle and sheep, that are driven to these places to be sold and sent forward to the south.
>
> At Sligachan the road was lined with tents. It was about eleven o'clock of the second day, and the tent-keepers were engaged in cooking broth, mutton, and potatoes for the country people inside, with the only drink, mountain dew.

Cattle that had been swum across from Skye often went on by way of Bealach Ratagain and up Glen Shiel to the Cluanie Inn, established in 1780. From here the route crossed the hills south-eastwards, dropping to the inn at Tomdoun on the River Garry, another resting point. Another route from the inn went by way of Fort Augustus and the Corrieyairack Pass to upper Strathspey, where stood the Pitmain Inn, a noted hostelry, which was located somewhere west of Kingussie. A very important cattle market, the Pitmain Tryst, was held here each September. It was followed by the Pitmain Ball, at which punch was freely drunk, speeches were delivered, and the Marquis of Huntly often sent a stag from the Gaick Forest for the meal. Elizabeth Grant noted in her *Memoirs of a Highland Lady* (1898) that lairds, drovers and farmers freely mingled, 'to enjoy the best good cheer the country afforded'. The inn later became an overnight stop on the coach route from Edinburgh to Inverness. Lord Cockburn was there when a coach arrived as he recollects in his journal of 1844: 'What a scene! Every monster rushed in and seized whatever he could lay his claws upon – meat, drink, the seat next the fire, the best room, the best bed – and awkwardness or timidity were left to shiver or starve!'

But by 1844 Cockburn noted that 'my old friend the inn of Pitmain I found converted into a farm-house'. 'Old friend' was a somewhat sarcastic comment, for in his journals he noted that it was 'an abominable hostel'.

After crossing Drumochter Pass the route headed south, across the grain of the land, past former inns at Trinafour and Tummel Bridge to the Coshieville Hotel, which stands five miles north-west of Aberfeldy, in Perthshire. This hotel is another that claims to be one of the county's oldest inns – in fact its advertisements maintain that it has been 'an inn for over one thousand years'. However, other accounts state that it was erected by General Wade as a barracks for his soldiers in the eighteenth century, and gunloops used to be visible on the fabric of the building (during a reconstruction in the 1930s these were covered up, and the old wooden bar that locked the door was removed). Various origins of the name Coshieville, which seems un-Scottish, have been put forward. One derives it from the French *cochons-ville*, as it is said that some French soldiers with General Wade lived like pigs; another links it with the Gaelic *coch a' bhil*, meaning 'at the foot of the sacred tree'.

One of the main drove routes south from Perthshire passed through Glen Devon. Cattle were driven up Glen Eagles, over the watershed into Glen Devon and thence south to the market at Falkirk. A popular resting place when passing down this valley was the Tormaukin Inn, or Hotel, and on the pastures around the hotel trysts, or markets, for sheep were at one time held. The name comes from the old Scots for 'hill of the mountain hare', and a white hare appears on the inn-sign. White-rendered, with black window surrounds, the two-storey inn is distinguished by its twin bay windows, which are later additions. An inn of some sort or other has stood here since the 1300s, but the present building probably

Tormaukin Hotel, Glendevon

dates from no earlier than around 1720. It has, however, been much altered and extended over the years. Today the inn is better known to the local sheep-farmers, although many golfers have visited the hostelry, including Nick Faldo and Colin Montgomery; Neil Armstrong and Burt Lancaster have also stayed there.

In Caithness, Sutherland and Ross and Cromarty there were also drove routes running southwards to join the other routes. In Sutherland there are a number of remote inns that owe their origin to the drovers but today are frequented by hill-walkers, fishermen and other sportsmen. One is the Crask Inn, which stands alone in Strath Tirry, the only building for miles around; two storeys in height, it dates from the late eighteenth century. Westwards, towards the head of Loch Shin, is the Overscaig Inn, again remotely situated. And, yet further west, the Inchnadamph Hotel at the head of

Loch Assynt was also founded as a drovers' inn. It has been much altered over the years, but its roots go back to 1736, when Murdoch MacKenzie – a drover himself, as well as the local tenant farmer – obtained a lease for the ground for thirty merks (about £1.66) plus one stone of tallow. (Tallow, rendered fat from sheep or cattle, was often used in the payment of leases for Highland inns and coaching houses.) A more substantial inn was erected in 1780, and it was extended as interest in natural history and sporting activities grew in the Victorian period; today it is much used by fishermen and hill-walkers.

From Inchnadamph the cattle were taken by way of Loch Shin to Bonar Bridge and Kincardine on the Dornoch Firth. South-west of Edderton, the Aultnamain Inn stands on the moorland road that runs from Bonar Bridge to Evanton – at one time a short-cut for south bound drovers, since it bypassed Tain and Alness, saving twelve miles, and led across open moorland, which reduced complaints from farmers and landowners about the amount of grazing consumed by the cattle. Five miles further down this road, near Stittenham, is a drove stance, where the cattle could be kept overnight. Stittenham Inn was built in 1835 by the Duke and Duchess of Sutherland (the name came from property they owned in Yorkshire) as one of their staging posts on the route north to Dunrobin Castle, but the building is no longer an inn.

Drovers who did not use the Aultnamain route could keep to the lower ground, by way of Tain and Milton. In the latter village stands the old Drovers' Inn, now converted into flats. It rises to two storeys and dates from the late eighteenth century. The journey continued by way of Dingwall and Beauly and thence over the Aird to Drumnadrochit and the Lewiston Arms, a drovers' inn of 1730.

The Loch Maree Hotel stands by the side of the loch of that name in Wester Ross, at the tiny clachan of Talladale. Queen Victoria's visit in October 1877 is commemorated by a Gaelic inscription on a large boulder. Whilst in the area the

Queen visited a waterfall just over a mile west of the hotel, ever since known as the Victoria Falls in her honour.

Cattle from Moray and Banffshire were often driven southwards through Aberdeenshire and Angus. The Pole Inn at Knockandhu near Tomintoul is a former drovers' rest, standing a storey and a half in height. From there the cattle were taken over the Leachd to the Forbes Arms at Cock Bridge, and then south by way of the former Rinloan Inn to Deeside. Another old Aberdeenshire inn frequented by the drovers lies a little further east. The Boultenstone Inn stands in hilly countryside between Strathdon and the Howe of Cromar, beside the present A 97 through Glen Deskry, which follows what used to be one of the most important droving routes in the county. 'Bouties' inn catered for the drovers' needs, being built to replace a much older hostelry nearby at Pantieland (said to derive from 'punder-land': a place where stray cattle were impounded). It was at Boultenstone Inn that 'Stachie' Laing died in 1838. He was a chapman who spent much of his time travelling round the district selling his publications; his *Donean Tourist* was popular in its day.

To the south of the Dee, five miles south-west of Banchory stands the Feughside Inn, now seemingly isolated but on what was once an important droving route from Deeside over the Cairn o' Mount to the south. Beside it, the Water of Feugh was crossed by an old five-arched bridge erected at the expense of the Rev. Dr Gilbert Ramsay of Barbados, until it was washed away in a flood in 1799 and had to be replaced. The Feughside Inn is mentioned in documents as early as 1549, though it is doubtful if any of the present building is so old.

Drove roads passed through many Perthshire villages, where there were inns ready to cater for the drovers' needs. The old inn at Woodside, south-west of Coupar Angus was one important resting place. A storey and a half in height, the Woodside Inn dates from the eighteenth century.

Droving also took place throughout the south-west of

Scotland, and drovers' inns survive in a number of places. Castle Douglas in the Stewartry of Kirkcudbright is still an important market town, and the Douglas Arms Hotel here is a former droving inn which has been in existence since at least 1779. A stone bearing this date, as well as the initials *WG MC*, can be seen on the wall facing King Street. Also on the wall of the hotel is a plaque, erected in 1827 and cast by J. Affleck of Dumfries, which details the mileages to various important towns – a must in droving days. Nearby towns are listed, ('Dumfries 18' and 'Gatehouse 15'), along with places further afield ('Edinburgh 90' and 'Glasgow 92'), but the inclusion of the English borough of Huntingdon, 290 miles away, is regarded by many as an unusual choice. However Huntingdon was an important destination for cattle-dealers, and it is thought that around 20,000 cattle annually were driven from this part of Scotland to the major tryst that took place there. They were then taken on to Norfolk to be fattened before sale in London markets (348 miles, according to the plaque). It is said that at one time, when the local laird was Sir William Douglas and the landlady of this inn was a Mrs Douglas, letters to the laird were often addressed to 'Sir William Douglas of Douglas Castle, care of Mrs Douglas, Douglas Arms, Castle Douglas'.

Cattle sold at Falkirk or Crieff were usually driven on south to the markets of England. A major drove route through the Lowlands and Southern Uplands can still be followed on the ground for much of its distance. At various places along it former drovers' inns survive, though today they have been updated, and their clientele has changed. At Leadburn, south of Penicuik, stands the Leadburn Inn, which dates back to 1777 when the Thomson family applied for a licence for 'the Privilege and Liberty of Brewing, Baking, Vending and Retailing Ales'. When the droving trade passed away the inn became a coaching stop and later – when the railway was built between Penicuik and Lanark (with a branch to Peebles), and Leadburn became an important junction – it benefited from yet another new mode of transport. Further south, in the Ettrick valley, is the Tushielaw Inn, a small inn standing by the side of what, in its day, was a major drove road from Peebles to Hawick. The Tushielaw was originally a toll-house and inn, and later developed as a coaching stop. The present building is Victorian in style, as a result of rebuilding.

The creation of military roads in Scotland by General Wade, General Caulfield and others in the eighteenth century was one of the tactics used by the British Government to help pacify the Highlands. These roads often followed the lines of drove routes, and as a result there was much animosity between drovers and the military road-builders – the drovers complained that the hard surface affected the cattle's hooves, and that landowners tried to restrict the cattle to the roads, thereby depriving them of the free grazing they had hitherto enjoyed. Where older inns either did not exist or were in a very poor condition, government-backed inns were built alongside these new military roads. They were to be run by landlords of an honest nature and were seen as being places where the weary traveller could safely spend the night; they were known as King's Houses, and a few of them retain this name. At first the buildings were used as camps or dormitories for the soldiers of General Wade and his successors who were employed in building the roads and bridges, but, when no longer required for this purpose, they were converted into inns. Wade established his camps at approximately ten-mile intervals, and their conversion to inns impressed a later road-builder, Thomas Telford, who wrote in the *Reports of Commissioners for Highland Roads and Bridges*:

A very important Consideration also is the erecting and maintaining of proper Inns upon the Roads. Several of the Houses which were built by the government upon the

Military Roads are striking instances of the necessity there is
of giving the People who are to keep the Inns something else
to depend on besides what arises from supplying Travellers;
there should be some land attached to the House.

The Kingshouse Hotel near Balquhidder, beside the A84,
two-and-a-half miles south of Lochearnhead, is an attractive
white-washed building with various extensions. The inn was
erected on the site of an ancient hunting lodge built in 1571
by King James VI of Scotland (later, from 1603, James I of
England) and subsequently owned by the Earl of Moray. This
old lodge was used by the soldiers as a base while the military
road was being constructed through the glen. On the 1
March 1779 a group of drovers, led by Patrick MacEwen,
John Robertson and Colin Robertson, submitted a lengthy
petition to the Land Commissioners for Scotland (who were
responsible for looking after the estates forfeited following
the 1745 rebellion) asking for an inn to be established in the
locality. The Commissioners agreed, and the inn was built at
a cost of £40. This Kingshouse had a cattle stance beside it
and was used primarily by drovers taking cattle from the
Highlands south towards Crieff and on to Falkirk.

In the mid-1770s the soldiers based at the Kingshouse were
responsible for killing a Balquhidder farmer. Rob Roy
MacGregor's son arranged to attack the building and cut the
Redcoats' throats, but the parish minister and others pleaded
with him not to carry out this deed; instead the minister
contacted the authorities and managed to obtain compensation for the farmer's widow and family. The inn is said to be
haunted, but no-one knows by whom or why. Graeme
Courtney, son of the proprietor, is one of a number of people
who have witnessed the spirit, but he could not verify
whether the manifestation had anything to do with this
murder.

Some twenty-five miles away on the A822, the Amulree
Hotel was originally established as a King's House when

General Wade's Military Road was built through the hills here in the 1730s. Amulree then became one of the most important staging posts for drovers heading south to Crieff via the Sma' Glen, and fairs were held in the village twice a year for the sale of cattle and sheep (an old cheese press stands in the hotel's garden). In 1803 William and Dorothy Wordsworth stopped for sustenance; the hotel has been much rebuilt since that time, however.

The Kingshouse Hotel on the Moor of Rannoch must be one of the most remote inns in Britain. Now by-passed by the main road, it stands on the desolate moor almost twelve miles from the nearest village, which lies at the foot of Glencoe.

In January 1692, just before the Massacre of Glencoe, it is said that the soldiers of the Earl of Argyll's Regiment, under Captain Campbell of Glenlyon, met at the inn to plan their attack. Colonel Hamilton was later stationed here with a large group of soldiers to search out and kill any surviving Macdonalds. However, he arrived on the scene rather late and, because of the weather, had to restrict his operations to looting and burning houses and stealing livestock, which he took to the garrison at Fort William.

The Kingshouse claims to be one of Scotland's oldest licensed inns, established in the seventeenth century, but the present building, and only part of that, probably dates from 1757, when the military road was pushed across the moor and over the Devil's Staircase towards Loch Linnhe. This work was carried out by General Caulfield's soldiers, who used the building as a barracks and rest-house.

At one time it was so difficult to keep the Kingshouse open that the government gave the landlord an annual grant and charged him no rent. But it was also noted as a haunt of salt smugglers; some of its landlords seem to have taken an active part in the trade. According to the poet Robert Southey, who stayed at the inn in 1819, one of the innkeepers made enough from the trade over ten years to purchase a farm and retire from inn-keeping; he had taken over the lease of the

Kingshouse in 1809 with a capital of £70, but by 1819 could buy a farm and stock it with £1,500 worth of cattle and sheep. At the end of the eighteenth century a single deal in contraband salt could net the smuggler a 200 per cent profit, because salt was in great demand and (apart from that used to preserve fish or export) was subject to a high rate of excise duty. It was thus a commodity suitable for smuggling, and the inn proved to be a convenient change-house for such trade. Southey notes, 'the excise officers give very little interruption to this trade, because the value of a seizure is far from being an adequate compensation for the trouble and risk of making it'. Southey had also spent the night at an inn in Fort Augustus and, on coming downstairs for breakfast, noted sitting behind the door six bags of salt that had been seized by the excisemen in the area.

Kingshouse, Rannoch Moor

The remoteness of the Kingshouse has not deterred visitors over the years; indeed, because it is the only place of refuge for many miles, it has attracted many travellers seeking sustenance and accommodation. Numerous accounts of travels through Scotland refer to the Kingshouse, and many early ones are less than complimentary. One of the earliest visitors was Thomas Pennant, who made *A Tour of Scotland* in 1769. He describes how he crossed the Devil's Staircase from Fort William to 'reach the King's House, seated in a plain: it was built for the accommodation of his Majesty's troops, in their march through this desolate country, but is in a manner unfurnished'. Thomas Newte stayed there in 1791, recording that it had 'not a bed in it for a decent person to sleep in, nor any provisions but what are absolutely necessary for the family'. When Southey paid a call he had a meal of mutton, but there was no bread in the place. He was offered 'turkey's eggs' (these may have been grouse eggs).

William and Dorothy Wordsworth stayed in 1803, the latter writing in her journal:

The house looked respectable at a distance – a large square building, cased in blue slates to defend it from storms – but when we came close to it the outside forewarned us of the poverty and misery within. Scarce a blade of grass could be seen growing upon the open ground ...

The first thing we saw on entering the door was two sheep hung up, as if just killed from the barren moor, their bones hardly sheathed in flesh. After we had waited a few minutes, looking about for a guide to lead us into some corner of the house, a woman, seemingly about forty years old, came to us in a great bustle, screaming in Erse, with the most horrible guinea-hen or peacock voice I ever heard, first to one person, then another. She could hardly spare time to show us up-stairs, for crowds of men were in the house – drovers, carriers, horsemen, travellers, all of whom she had to provide with supper, and she was, as she told us, the only woman there.

Never did I see such a miserable, such a wretched place – long rooms with ranges of beds, no other furniture except benches, or perhaps one or two crazy chairs, the floors far dirtier than an ordinary house could be if it were never washed … as dirty as a house after a sale on a rainy day, and the rooms being large and the walls naked they looked as if more than half the goods had been sold out.

We sat shivering in one of the large rooms for three-quarters of an hour before the woman could find time to speak to us again; she then promised a fire in another room, after two travellers, who were going a stage further, had finished their whisky, and said we should have supper as soon as possible. She had no eggs, no milk, no potatoes, no loaf-bread, or we should have preferred tea. With length of time the fire was kindled, and, after another hour's waiting, supper came – a shoulder of mutton so hard that it was impossible to chew the little flesh that might be scraped off the bones, and some sorry soup made of barley and water, for it had no other taste.

After supper, the woman, having first asked if we slept on blankets, brought in two pair of sheets, which she begged that I would air by the fire, for they would be dirtied below-stairs. I was very willing, but behold! the sheets were so wet, that it would have been at least a two-hours' job before a far better fire than could be mustered at King's House.

In June 1804 James Hogg stayed at the Kingshouse during one of his Highland tours. He noted that:

The day was very hot, and we arrived at the King's House, in the Black Mount, almost parched with thirst – 'Have you any porter?' said Mr L. on entering, – 'haneal', said the wife, – 'And ale?' said he – 'Oh! That's very good'. We were very sorry to find she had answered in Gaelic, and that she has neither the one nor the other. She had, however, plenty of tea, the only beverage in the Highlands that a stranger can partake of freely.

In 1903 Alexander Wilkie stayed at Kingshouse and noted that he received:

a hearty welcome. Tea, my clothes and shoes dried. Next
morning after a walk round I go in for breakfast. What shall I
have? – grapefruit? What! can I have grapefruit in
Kingshouse; of course I can; and so I have grapefruit, and
porridge and cream, and fish, and everything just like a west
end city hotel. I tell you I am well looked after and at a charge
so moderate that I am almost ashamed of my appetite.

J.H.B. Bell, a noted Scots climber and writer, used the
Kingshouse as a base for his expeditions in the 1920s. He
wrote that, 'from one's bedroom one could smell the bacon
frying through a hole in the floor, which was better than a
breakfast gong. In another room it was said to be necessary
to put up an umbrella in bed if the weather was wet, which
was very often the case'.

The Kingshouse appears in a number of novels. These
include *The New Road* by Neil Munro, *Kidnapped* by Robert
Louis Stevenson and *Children of the Dead End* by Patrick
MacGill. *The New Road* (1919) is set in the period when the
military roads were being built, and the chapter entitled 'The
Inn at Buachaille Etive' describes the location: 'The tavern
crouched, low-eaved and black, beside a pack-horse bridge
on Rannoch edge, and not another light except its own in all
the evening.' *Kidnapped* (1886) was based on the story of the
Appin Murder of 1752. *Children of the Dead End* (1982) is
an 'autobiographical novel' set in the first decade of the
twentieth century, when the Blackwater dam was being built
to create the large reservoir that now lies above Kinlochleven.
Navvies brought in to work on the dam had to live in huts,
and even in the winter snowstorms were so desperate for a
drink that they braved the elements and crossed the Devil's
Staircase to the Kingshouse and back, a round trip of twelve
miles. Tales abound of corpses being discovered in the spring
thaws, still holding their bottles of whisky close to their
chest!

Drovers used the Kingshouse as one of their main

overnight stops en route to Crieff. The grazing rights to the ground next to the inn are still held by the Glencoe crofters, and the stance where the cattle were once kept overnight still produces lusher grass than the bleak surroundings.

The Loch Ericht Hotel at Dalwhinnie (formerly known as the Dalwhinnie Hotel) has its origins as a King's House. The southern part of the building was put up by Wade's men, though a large modern extension has been added. It was described in 1812 by Elizabeth Grant as a 'good inn', and when Queen Victoria and Prince Albert stayed here on 8 October 1861 the Queen wrote in her journal:

> The inn of Dalwhinnie ... stands by itself, away from any village. Here, again, there were a few people assembled, and I thought they knew us; but it seems they did not, and it was only when we arrived that one of the maids recognised me. She had seen me at Aberdeen and Edinburgh. We went upstairs: the inn was much larger than at Fettercairn, but not nearly so nice and cheerful; there was a drawing-room and a dining-room; and we had a very good-sized bedroom. Albert had a dressing-room of equal size ... unfortunately there was hardly anything to eat, and there was only tea, and two miserable starved Highland chickens, without any potatoes! No pudding, and no *fun*; no little maid.... It was not a nice supper; and the evening was wet.

At Whitebridge, nine miles north-east of Fort Augustus along General Wade's Military Road stands another King's House. On older maps named the Whitebridge Inn, it is now known as the Whitebridge Hotel. There were also King's Houses that are now lost, abandoned or converted that once existed at Aonach, Aviemore, Dalmagarry, Dalnacardoch, Dulsie Bridge, Garbhamór, Moulinearn, Old Blair, Shiel House, Trinafour, and Tummel Bridge. The Aonach inn, which Johnson and Boswell visited on their jaunt round the Highlands, must have been situated somewhere in Glen

Garbhamór Kingshouse, Inverness-shire

Moriston, between the Torgyle and Ceannacroc bridges. The Kingshouse at Aviemore was visited in 1786 for the second time by Colonel T. Thornton, and he wrote that, 'it hurts me to say that I found the inn I now put up at differing from those I had passed, it being but very indifferently kept; the rooms very dirty; whereas when I was here before no inn could be in better order'. The Dalmagarry inn near Moy, is now a farm. It had originally been built in 1732, a two-storey building with four rooms, but in the aftermath of Culloden in 1746 it was partially destroyed by fire.

The former inns at Dalnacardoch and Old Blair, in Atholl in Perthshire, were visited by Queen Victoria on one of her jaunts; Dalnacardoch will be mentioned in more detail in Chapter 6, while Old Blair was later converted into the Atholl estate factor's house. The Trinafour inn was at the bridge over the Errochty, ten miles west of Blair Atholl. Shiel House at the head of Loch Duich was visited by James Hogg, but Robert Southey noted in 1819 that 'this inn, built by Government solely for the accommodation of travellers in these western wilds' was now closed. Dulsie Bridge Kingshouse still stands by the side of the River Findhorn in Nairnshire, but it has been converted into a private house, but the Garbhamór Kingshouse is in ruins – although two of its old box-beds are kept in the West Highland Museum at Fort William (one is labelled 'General Wade's bed'). The Moulinearn inn still stands three miles down Strathtummel from Pitlochry, but it has long been converted into a farm. It was here Sir Alexander Mackenzie, the explorer of the Canadian north, died in 1820; taken ill while travelling north from Edinburgh to his home at Avoch, he was carried to the inn but died soon after. The Tummel Bridge Kingshouse, five miles from Trinafour, at the west end of Loch Tummel has been converted into a private house.

A building at Letterfinlay, beside Loch Lochy, is said to have been built by Wade's soldiers as quarters for the officers in charge of building the road from Fort Augustus to Fort William. When the soldiers left it was turned into an inn and was a popular resting place for drovers. The building was later converted into the mansion house of Letterfinlay estate, but around 1875, when the later shooting lodge was erected, it became a farmer's house.

It was not only rural inns that drovers frequented. Some inns in Glasgow and Edinburgh were noted for their custom from drovers – though usually when they were on their way back north, without their cattle – and many tales were no doubt told about their exploits on the journey south, and the sums realized at the markets probably increased in the telling as the drink flowed! A notable drovers' inn used to stand in Dumbarton Road in Glasgow, its site now occupied by the Thornwood roundabout; known as Granny Gibb's Cottage, it was run by Elizabeth Gibb and her daughters. In Edinburgh Captain Edward Topham noted a city-centre inn used by drovers in 1774. When shown into the tap room by a girl he found 'about twenty Scotch drovers ... regaling themselves with whisky and potatoes'.

5   Writers' Rests

The convivial atmosphere and good company provided by the inn seem to have attracted poets and authors over the centuries. Many writers have found the 'crack' by the inn's fireside conducive to good writing, and dozens of famous works have been conceived there. Virtually all Scotland's notable writers have frequented inns, leaving behind a tale to tell of their visit. Burns, Scott, Stevenson, to name but three of the best known, have all been associated with several inns – but so, too, have a good many others, as we shall see.

The Ayrshire poet and national bard, Robert Burns (1759–96) was a regular visitor to a number of inns throughout the south-west, as he moved from Alloway to Mauchline to Dumfries. Many of his locals still survive, and other inns where he spent the odd night, either on his tours or else on business, still have memories of his times there.

Just up the road from his birthplace at Alloway, in the county town of Ayr, stands the Tam o' Shanter Inn in the High Street. The inn was built around 1748, when Janet Kennedy was its tenant, but in 1808 it was rebuilt and occupied as a house by James Shearer. The building probably has no direct links with the poet (nor with Douglas Graham, the original Tam o' Shanter), and it is not known whether or not he ever paid it a call, but a nineteenth-century landlord changed its name from the Plough Inn to that of the hero of Burns' poem 'Tam o' Shanter' and advertised the building as 'the house where Tam o' Shanter and Souter Johnnie held their meetings'. This proved to be a great advertising gimmick and the salvation of the old inn, for it survives in the middle of a busy shopping centre, still with its thatched roof (typical of the type of building that formerly lined the High Street). In 1944 the inn was purchased by the town council and converted into a museum of artefacts associated with Burns and his period, which remained as such until around 1990, when the building was closed because of its dangerous condition. After lying empty for a couple of years it was restored and reopened as a public house in 1993.

Burns' poem describes the scene at the inn:

> But to our tale: – Ae market night,
> Tam had got planted unco right,
> Fast by an ingle, bleezing finely,
> Wi' reaming swats, that drank divinely,
> And at his elbow, Souter Johnie,
> His ancient, trusty, drouthy cronie:
> Tam lo'ed him like a very brither,
> They had been fou for weeks thegither.
> The night drave on wi sangs and clatter,
> And ay the ale was growing better:
> The landlady and Tam grew gracious,
> Wi' secret favours, sweet and precious:
> The Souter tauld his queerest stories;
> The landlord's laugh was ready chorus:
> The storm without might rair and rustle,
> Tam did na mind the storm a whistle.

When Burns married Jean Armour they set up home in a house in Castle Street, Mauchline, a building that still survives and contains a museum. Just across the narrow street stands Nanse Tannock's Inn, built in 1712 and originally named the Small Inn, but now long closed. Here Burns sometimes spent his idle hours, but another inn in the village, which still operates as such, also has associations with the poet. Poosie Nansie's stands in Loudoun Street, at the junction with the Cowgate, and is supposed to date from 1700. In Burns's time it had a rather poor reputation, for the landlord, George Gibson, kept a disorderly house, his wife (Poosie Nansie) was a regular drunk, and their daughter was convicted of receiving stolen goods. When called before the kirk session in 1773, charged with being drunk too often and disruptive to her neighbours, Poosie Nansie went to the kirk, only to tell the elders that she intended to continue in her wayward ways! Robert Burns used Poosie Nansie's as the setting for his poem 'The Jolly Beggars', which contains the lines:

> Ae night at e'en a merry core o' randie, gangrel bodies
> In Poosie Nansie's held the splore, to drink their orra
>   duddies.

Today Poosie Nansie's Inn (or Tavern, as it is sometimes called) is still a popular refreshment place in the village. It also contains a few relics associated with the poet and his friends. Just across the Cowgate from the inn a plaque marks the site of the Whitefoord Arms, an inn more frequented by Burns.

Further down Mauchline's Loudoun Street stands the red-sandstone Loudoun Arms. Known at the time as John MacLelland's Inn, this was also visited by Burns, who in 1786 attended a reading club here. The hotel is now home to Mauchline Burns Club, established in 1923. It is also known in the district as the pub where you can get a free drink – this is not an alcoholic drink, but a drop of pure spring water. On the façade of the inn runs what is known as the Loudoun Spoot, continually flowing night and day with water from Ayrshire's oldest artesian well.

On the road down Nithsdale towards Dumfries we find the Auldgirth Inn, a quaint-looking building situated at the north end of the old bridge (erected in 1782 – now by-passed). The inn is distinguished by its gothic-arched windows and crosses on the chimney, giving it a somewhat ecclesiastical air. This inn was used by Burns as a resting place on his way from Dumfriesshire to Ayrshire.

In Dumfries are three surviving old inns associated with Burns. The Globe Inn at 56 High Street was established in 1610, and was noted by the bard as 'my howff'. On an upstairs window he is said to have scratched some lines in praise of 'Lovely Polly Stewart' and a version of 'Coming Through the Rye'. It was here that Burns composed the lines entitled 'Grace before and after meat', supposedly as the result of an incident when he intended to book a meal there, but forgot to do so. When he arrived with his two friends, the landlord John Hyslop and his wife Meg gave up their own meal for them. However, his friend Willie Nicol is said to have 'fined' Burns by asking him to compose a grace. Burns extemporised:

> O Lord, since we have feasted thus,
>   Which we so little merit,
> Let Meg now take away the flesh,
>   And Jock bring in the spirit!

Later in life, as Burns neared his death, he was left in the embarrassing situation of owing money to the Hyslops, and he asked his publishers, James Johnson, to help out.

Meg Hyslop's niece, Helen Park, worked at the Globe for a time as a barmaid. She and Burns had an affair when his wife was absent, which resulted in the birth of a daughter, Elizabeth, in 1791. Helen seems to have died soon after the birth. The affair resulted in the song 'Yestreen I had a Pint o' Wine'. (Burns's wife, who gave birth to a son nine days later, seems to have taken in the girl and brought her up as her own, claiming that 'Oor Robbie should ha'e had twa wives'.) The ghost of Helen Park – or Anna as she is referred to in

Globe Tavern, Dumfries

Burns's poetry – is said to haunt the inn. Reports of her appearance have been made over the centuries, but a recent sighting took place in 1996 when a waitress saw a figure dressed in an old-fashioned full-skirted dress ascending the stairs at considerable speed. The shocked waitress, Kirsty Mawhinney, reported the sighting to the dining-room manageress, but following an inspection upstairs no sign of anything was found.

Later visitors to the Globe included Robert Louis Stevenson, Rudyard Kipling, Woodrow Wilson, Andrew Carnegie and J.M. Barrie, all of whom signed the inn's impressive visitors' book. A visitor who kept himself to himself, was the travel writer H.V. Morton, author of *In Search of Scotland* (1929) who wrote an admirable description of the inn on a 'song-night'. Returning whilst writing *In Scotland Again* (1933), he again visited incognito. A young man advised Morton to read his own book, and the landlord leaned over the bar and announced, 'He was here in this very room!'

In the 1930s the Globe was bought by M. Henry MacKerrow, President of the Burns Federation from 1937 until 1943, who was anxious to preserve the old inn. He and his family, who still run it, have built up a small collection of artefacts associated with the bard. These include the poet's chair, punch-bowl, jug and ladle.

A second Dumfries inn that Burns is thought to have used on occasions is the Hole i' the Wa' Inn (Hole in the Wall), which lies between the High Street and Queensberry Street. According to a surviving marriage lintel, which commemorates James Haike and Jean Stot, the building dates from 1620. In the late nineteenth century the landlord, John Thomson, converted the bar into what was virtually a museum of Burns relics, making it a popular place of pilgrimage for tourists; his collection included Burns's burgess ticket, bought at auction in 1904 for £55. The relics have been transferred to the Robert Burns Centre in the town but the inn is still in use as a public bar.

Another of the many inns in Dumfries associated with Burns is located at the junction of the Whitesands with Friars Vennel. Today known as Granville's, it was originally called the Coach and Horses and was often frequented by drovers and travellers who came to Dumfries market. The inn had a reputation as a brothel, for upstairs Margaret King or Hog, whom Burns called 'Muirland Meg', kept an indecent house that was infamous for miles around. Across the Nith in the formerly separate town of Maxwelltown – originally in a different county but today basically a suburb of Dumfries – stands the George Inn, an old hostelry where Burns is known to have drunk.

From Dumfries Burns made a tour of Galloway, in the course of which he stayed in Kirkcudbright, county town of the Stewartry. Here, on 1 August 1793, he is thought to have said the 'Selkirk Grace' for the first time. Some say that this took place at lunchtime in the Selkirk Arms (formerly known as the Heid Inn), but others say that the grace was not spoken until later that day, when he dined at St Mary's Isle with Lord Selkirk.

Some hae meat and canna eat,
And some wad eat that want it;
But we hae meat and we can eat,
And sae the Lord be thankit.

The Selkirk Arms first opened in 1750 (or 1770, as some accounts have it) but it did not receive its licence to sell liquor until 1777. Burns stayed here many times whilst working as an exciseman, and on one occasion seems to have composed a poem on the wall of his room. During renovations layers of old wallpaper were stripped off, and underneath was found a sketch of a church and four lines of a poem signed 'R. Burns'; these were an early draft of 'The Lass that Made the Bed to Me'.

West along the Galloway coast from Kirkcudbright is the attractive village of Gatehouse-of-Fleet. Here stands the Murray Arms Hotel, an old posting inn established in 1642 that has been extended over the years. The oldest part, which faces what used to be the main street through the village (now Ann Street), was the original 'gait house' that marked the edge of Cally Park. Old feu charters make reference to this building as an inn; the building was part of Cally estate, whose owner, James Murray of Broughton and Cally, laid out a planned village here in the 1760s. The other main section of the Murray Arms dates from this time and faces the present main street. Here, on 31 July 1793, Robert Burns and John Syme spent the night while touring Galloway. During his stay Burns wrote the stirring song 'Scots Wha Ha'e wi' Wallace bled' (for many years regarded as the national anthem of Scotland), which the poet originally titled 'Robert Bruce's March to Bannockburn', and the room where the lines were written is known today as the Burns Room. The Murray Arms is also thought to be the original of the 'Gordon Arms at Kippletringan' in Sir Walter Scott's tale of smuggling and excisemen, *Guy Mannering*; part of the action takes place in the kitchen of the inn, described as 'a small but

Murray Arms Hotel, Gatehouse-of-Fleet

comfortable inn, kept by Mrs MacCandlish'. The Murray
Arms is still part of Cally Estate, and, following a complete
renovation, won a Civic Trust Amenity Award in 1959.

Five Red Herrings is a murder-mystery novel in the Lord
Peter Wimsey series, written by Dorothy L. Sayers
(1893–1957) and first issued in 1931. Set in the Galloway
countryside, the tale has associations with the Anwoth Hotel
in Gatehouse-of-Fleet. This hostelry, which has been rebuilt
and extended over the years, was formerly known as the Ship
Inn, for Gatehouse was at one time quite a busy port.

In the Lanarkshire village of Carnwath we can see a
thatched inn, one of few surviving in Scotland. The Wee Bush
Inn dates from 1750 and is distinguished by its red-painted

doors and window-surrounds. It was visited by Burns in 1786, and it is thought that he may have scratched his motto, 'Better a Wee Bush than Nae Bield' on a window here – hence the inn's name.

In the Gallowgate of Glasgow is the Saracen's Head. The present building was erected only in 1905, but it replaced an ancient inn which was celebrated in the folklore of the city. In the eighteenth century the city had no hotels as such, only small inns and ale-houses, and the visitor had either to risk staying at one of these or else be put up by a 'stabler', who was more geared up for looking after their horses! Vintner Robert Tennant applied to the city magistrates for permission to erect a hotel in the Bridgeton area, and the council encouraged him in his venture. The original inn, three storeys high, was erected in 1754, and the stone was taken from the ruined Bishop's Palace, next to Glasgow Cathedral, and from the old Gallowgate Port (which Tennant was allowed to demolish in return for paying the city treasurer £10). The name was copied from the famous Saracen's Head Hotel in London. Robert Tennant died in 1757; his widow Katherine took over the lease, at fifty guineas per annum, and when she died the inn was sold to James Graham. Tennant's family went on to found the Tennant Brewery, which today has grown into one of the largest brewers in the country.

In the *Glasgow Courant* of October 1755 the opening of the 36-bedroom inn was heralded:

Robert Tennant, who formerly kept the White Hart Inn, without the Gallowgate Port, is removed to the Saracen's Head, where the port formerly stood. He takes this opportunity to acquaint all ladies and gentlemen, that at the desire of the magistrates of Glasgow, he has built a convenient and handsome new inn, agreeable to a plan given him, containing 36 fine rooms, now fit to receive lodgers. The bed-chambers are all separate, none of them entering through another, and so contrived that there is no need of going out of doors to get to them. The beds are all very good, clean and free from bugs. There are very good stables for horses, and a pump well in the yard for watering them, with a shade within the said yard for coaches, chaises, or other wheel carriages.

The inn became the terminus for the London coach (a blunderbuss, carried for protection against highwaymen, is preserved in the present inn) and was the scene of many notable events and functions in the city, for it had a ballroom that could accommodate a hundred dancers. The stables had room for sixty horses and numerous carriages. The inn had such a high reputation for service that many local lairds and merchants sent their daughters there for 'lessons in the culinary arts'. A blue-and-white glazed Delftfield punch bowl that belonged to the inn, and which can hold almost five gallons, is preserved in the People's Palace Museum on Glasgow Green; it is reckoned to date from around 1760 and is adorned with the Glasgow arms and the motto *Success to the Town of Glasgow*. The bowl was sold at the same time as the inn in 1791, and passed down to John Buchanan who left it to the museum in 1910 (it had been last used in 1860 at a public dinner held by the Glasgow Archaeological Society).

Virtually every person of rank or note who had reason to visit the city stayed at the Saracen's Head. Johnson and Boswell stayed in October 1773, John Wesley called, and Robert Burns paid a visit in 1788, the same year as the first London coach. Samuel Taylor Coleridge, Dorothy and William Wordsworth stayed for two days in 1803 – Dorothy noting that it was 'quiet and tolerably cheap, a new building' – and the poet James Hogg, the 'Ettrick Shepherd', stayed in May 1804. An early account of the inn noted that:

On the arrival of the mail at the Saracen's Head, all the idlers of the city crowded around it and at the door stood two visitors 'who were specially selected for their handsome appearance' with embroidered coats, red plush breeches, and powdered hair. When the Judges, or the sporting Duke of Hamilton, were expected, the waiters got themselves up in still more ornate style, and even mounted silk stockings. On these occasions, they were looked up to with awe, wonder and respect by all the urchins of the neighbourhood.

The Saracen's Head fell on evil days as the nineteenth century progressed. The main hub of the city had moved further west, and new and bigger hotels stole its trade. It was divided into tenements and became so rotten that in 1904 it was sold for demolition. When it was taken down the following year workmen discovered skeletons below the floor. On investigation it was discovered that the inn had been built on the site of the ancient kirkyard of Little St Mungo's Chapel, which had been converted into a leper hospital in the 1600s (a skull from the burial is on display in the present inn – it belonged to a fifteen-year-old girl who died of leprosy). The remains of St Mungo's Well were restored in 1906 (Christian converts were said to have met St Kentigern – or Mungo – here on his return from Wales), and tradition has it that this spot is where Glasgow's patron saint met St Columba.

On visits to Glasgow in June 1787 and in February and March 1788 Robert Burns stayed not at the Saracen's Head but at the Black Bull Inn, which stood at the junction of Argyle and Virginia Streets on a site now occupied by a large shop. A plaque, erected by the Scottish Burns Club, commemorates this fact. It was here that Burns wrote his love epistle to 'Clarinda'. The Black Bull had been built in 1758 by the Highland Society of Glasgow and had stabling for 38 horses. The story goes that, when the evangelist George Whitefield preached to a large congregation in the cathedral burial ground, a collection taken at the suggestion of the society raised enough to fund the building of the inn.

Black Bull Inn, Glasgow

William and Dorothy Wordsworth toured Scotland in 1803, staying at a number of inns on the way. In the Border country they spent the night at the Mosspaul Inn, in the hills between Langholm and Hawick, an old coaching inn built on the site of a hospice run by the monks of Melrose Abbey, where a small chapel formerly stood. Dorothy described the location:

The scene, with this single dwelling, was melancholy and wild, but not dreary, though there was no tree nor shrub; the small streamlet glittered, the hills were populous with sheep; but the gentle bending of the valley, and the correspondent softness in the forms of the hills, were of themselves enough to delight the eye.

Each year at the Mosspaul Inn the cornets of the towns of Langholm and Hawick meet. These officials, who play an important part in the annual riding of the marches of each community, each ride their horses about ten miles to meet at the inn and exchange greetings.

The Wordsworths then moved on to Hawick, where they put up at the Tower Inn. This incorporated on one side a castle, known as Drumlanrig's Tower, which was erected in the sixteenth century by William Douglas and by around 1773 was converted into the main inn of the town. The Tower Inn remained in business until the 1970s, but in recent years has been converted into a museum and information centre, with the old tower restored. It reopened to tourists in 1995. The building bears a plaque commemorating the writers' visit on 22 September 1803 (when Sir Walter Scott also stayed there). They also stayed at the White Hart Inn in Edinburgh's Grassmarket, which they described as cheap but noisy. This old coaching hostelry had already been visited by Robert Burns in 1791, on his last trip to the capital (a plaque over an adjoining close commemorates the event). The building dates from the eighteenth century and is distinguished by its wallhead gables (a series of small gables facing the street) and broken pediment, bearing a representation of a white hart; in its hey-day it was an important meeting place for gentry and lairds from around the country who were in Edinburgh on business.

In the village of Roslin, just south of Edinburgh, stands the Rosslyn Inn, which now calls itself the 'Old Original Rosslyn Hotel'. It was converted into a private house, named Collegehill House, for a number of years but is once more a popular hostelry. Parts of the building date from 1660, and it still contains early eighteenth-century cut-out balusters on the main staircase, though most of the present building dates from 1827. A plaque on the wall, erected in 1950, records part of the inn's history:

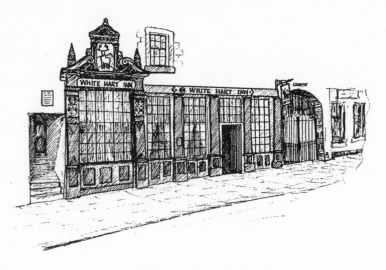

White Hart Inn, Edinburgh

The old Rosslynn Inn (circa 1660–1866).
Here countless travellers tarried awhile.
Among the distinguished visitors were
King Edward VII, when Prince of Wales,
Dr Samuel Johnson and James Boswell,
Robert Burns and Alexander Naysmith,
Sir Walter Scott and William and Dorothy
Wordsworth

Missing from the list is Queen Victoria, who was here in
1856, and King George V and Queen Mary, who paid a visit
in 1931 and identified an inscription on a window: 'Prince
Edward dined here on the anniversary of his mother's
birthday, 1854.' Robert Burns visited with Alexander
Nasmyth (as his name is more usually spelled) and
breakfasted at the inn; Nasmyth, one of the most important
Scottish painters of his time, was noted for his landscapes and
also for his portrait of Burns. The bard wrote on one of the
inn's windows, and also inscribed a pewter plate:

My blessings on ye, honest wife,
I ne'er was here before;
Ye've wealth o' gear for spoon and knife –
Heart could not wish for more.

Heav'n keep you clear o' sturt and strife,
Till far ayont fourscore,
And by the Lord o' death and life,
I'll ne'er gae by your door.

Johnson and Boswell 'dined and drank tea at the inn' in November 1773, on their way south after their tour of the Highlands and Hebrides. The Wordsworths visited in September 1803, en route back to England from their Highland tour; they walked from the inn to Lasswade, where Sir Walter Scott lived at the time.

Sir Walter Scott has associations with a number of old inns. One of them, the Gordon Arms, lying in the countryside at a crossroads in the vale of Yarrow, has long been a favourite haunt of fishermen and tourists. Rising to two storeys, it is finished in the typical Scots manner and was built in the first part of the nineteenth century by John Gordon, a contractor to the Duke of Buccleuch. (According to a licence application of 21 May 1828, which still survives at the hotel, 'John Gordon has always behaved civilly and honourably to his customers'; the application includes James Hogg as a referee.) It was here that Scott and Hogg parted company for the last time in the autumn of 1830, and a plaque on the wall commemorates the event. According to Hogg, Scott sent him word that he was to pass by en route from Drumlanrig to Abbotsford:

I accordingly waited at the inn and handed him out of the carriage. His daughter was with him, but we left her at the inn, and walked slowly down the way as far as Mount Benger Burn. He then walked very ill indeed, for the weak limb had become almost completely useless; but he leaned on my shoulder all the way, and did me the honour of saying that he never leaned on a firmer or a surer. We talked of many things, past, present, and to come, but both his memory and onward calculation appeared to me then to be considerably decayed. I cannot tell what it was, but there was something in his manner that distressed me. He often changed the subject very abruptly, and never laughed. He expressed the deepest concern for my welfare and success in life more than I had ever heard him do before, and all mixed with sorrow for my worldly misfortunes. There is little doubt that his own were then preying on his vitals. When I handed him into the coach that day, he said something to me which, in the confusion of parting, I forgot; and though I tried to recollect the words the next minute, I could not, and never could again. It was something to the purport that it was likely it would be long ere he leaned as far on my shoulder again. But there was an expression in it, conveying his affection for me, or his interest in me, which has escaped my memory for ever.

In Selkirk, where Scott presided as Sheriff of the county from 1799 to 1832 and where his statue stands in the square, is the County Hotel. The novelist often visited this hotel to attend functions, and it was here that he persuaded his daughter Sophia to sing the Souters' song to the assembled audience. A historic coaching halt, the County was also patronized by James Hogg, Robert Southey and the Duke of Wellington over the years. Elsewhere in Selkirk a plaque on a wall marks the 'site of old Forest Inn where Burns wrote his Epistle to Willie Creech 13th May 1787'.

The Clovenfords Hotel in the village of the same name, near Galashiels in the Borders, is an old coaching inn of around 1750 that has been pleasantly converted to a quiet country inn. In the early nineteenth century it was regularly visited by Sir Walter Scott when he had to travel from his home, which was at that time in Lasswade, to his work at

Selkirk. Whilst lodging here he wrote some of his early major poetry, 'Marmion' and 'The Lady of the Lake'. The inn was also visited by William and Dorothy Wordsworth, and William mentioned it in 'Yarrow Revisited'.

> And with the Tweed had travelled,
> And when we came to Clovenford,
> Then said my winsome marrow,
> 'Whate'er betide we'll turn aside,
> And see the Braes of Yarrow.'

The inn closed in 1833, but reopened in 1901 and has remained in business ever since. In 1911 a statue of Sir Walter Scott was erected in front of the inn. This figure, carved by J. Archibald of Galashiels, was originally used in a gala there, but no place for it could be found in the town, so it was erected at Clovenfords, (with a £100 annuity to ensure its preservation). The Clovenfords Hotel is said to be haunted, for some have seen the dim image of an unidentified man with a dog passing through walls and furniture.

Tibbie Shiels Inn stands in a romantic position on a low neck of land between St Marys Loch and the Loch o' the Lowes, deep in the Border hills between Moffat and Selkirk. Originally a cottage on the estate of Lord Napier, this was the home of molecatcher Robert Richardson and his wife Isabella Shiel. She was left a young widow in 1823 and, in order to survive, began selling ale and other refreshments to travellers. The cottage's location, and Tibbie's charm, made it a popular stopping-off point. Her first guest is said to have been Robert Chambers, who was collecting material for *Picture of Scotland*. Such was Tibbie's attention that he suggested that she open her house as an inn. In his book Chambers wrote:

> There has lately been erected at the head of the Loch a small, neat house, kept by a decent shepherd's widow, who lets her spare room for any length of time at a small rent, and who can

provide her lodgers with as wholesome and agreeable country fare as may anywhere be found. It is hardly possible to conceive anything more truly delightful than a week's ruralizing in this comfortable little mansion, with the means of so much amusement at the very doors, and so many interesting objects of sight and sentiment lying closely around.

Soon it became well-known as the haunt of the Border and Edinburgh literary aristocracy, and visitors came from miles around. Writers included Sir Walter Scott, James Hogg, the journalist John Wilson (who wrote as 'Christopher North' and set at least one scene in the 'Noctes Ambrosianae' here), Thomas de Quincey, John Gibson Lockhart, William Edmondstoune Aytoun, Thomas Carlyle, Henry Glassford Bell, Robert Louis Stevenson, Alexander Russel (editor of the *Scotsman*), Thomas Tod Stoddart (the 'king of angler rhymers') and many others. Men of religion, such as John Caird, John Cairns, Thomas Chalmers and Thomas Guthrie, visited, and among the academics and politicians were Sir David Brewster – inventor of the kaleidoscope and other lens-based items – and William Ewart Gladstone. Hogg described the inn as 'a cosy bield, this o' Tibbie's – just like a wee bit wren's nest', and the novelist David Pae wrote in the visitors' book for 1867:

> Oh, what are all the pomp and pride
> Of feudal lords of high degree
> Compar'd with Tibbie's clean fireside,
> And ingle bleezing bonnielie?

The inn building at Tibbie Shiel's dates from the early nineteenth century, though it has been extended several times, including in 1945; the original cot-house is still attached to the greater hotel. Near to the inn stands a statue of one of its first landlady's most famous customers, James Hogg, gazing over the peaceful waters of the loch. Tibbie

Shiel died in 1878 in her 96th year and is buried in Ettrick kirkyard where her tombstone can still be seen, but it is said that she still haunts the hostelry. She is rarely seen, however, and is usually just 'felt' forcing her way towards the fire, as she was wont to do when she was alive. There is also said to be a second spirit, that of a dog that belonged to the proprietor at the turn of the century. His master died when away on business, and the dog died of starvation before being found.

The Middleton Inn, which stands beside the A7, south of Gorebridge, was a coaching inn, located one stage out from the centre of Edinburgh, a distance of twelve miles. It was popular with people travelling between the Borders and the city on business. Sir Walter Scott regularly rested here, where he became friendly with the landlady Mrs Wilson (at a time when he feared that he would go to prison on account of the debts he was responsible for, he noted in his journal, 'Ah, good Mrs Wilson, you know not you are like to lose an old customer'). Lord Cockburn, a noted circuit judge who kept a detailed journal of his times, wrote about a typical evening's entertainment at the Middleton Inn in his youth. It was his very first visit to an inn:

> We returned to the Inn at Middleton, on our way home, about seven in the evening, and there we saw another scene which I have never forgotten. People sometimes say that there is no probability in Scott's making the party in *Waverley* retire from the Castle to the Howf; but these people were not with me at the inn at Middleton, about fifty years ago [circa 1780]. The Duke of Buccleuch was living at Dalkeith; Henry Dundas, then Home Secretary, at Melville; Robert Dundas, the Lord Advocate, at Arniston; Hepburn of Clerkington at Middleton; and several of the rest of the aristocracy of Midlothian within a few miles off; all with their familes, and luxurious houses; yet they, to the number of twelve or sixteen, congregated in this wretched ale-house for a day of freedom

and jollity. We found them roaring and singing, and laughing, in a low-roofed room scarcely large enough to hold them, with wooden chairs and sanded floor. When their own lacqueys, who were carrying on high life in the kitchen, did not choose to attend, the masters were served by two women. There was plenty of wine, particularly claret, in rapid circulation on the table; but my eye was attracted by a huge bowl of hot whisky punch, the steam of which was almost dripping from the roof, while the odour was enough to perfume the whole parish. We were called in and made to partake, and were very kindly used, particularly by my uncle Harry Dundas. How they did joke and laugh! with songs and toasts, and disputation, and no want of practical fun! I don't remember anything they said, and probably did not understand it. But the noise, and the heat, and the uproarious mirth, I think I hear and feel yet.

Lord Cockburn also noted that the original inn was no longer in existence by 1839, for it was rebuilt in 1790 and the site of the old howf marked by 'a square of ash trees'.

In 1817 Sir Walter Scott made a tour of Lennox, in particular Loch Lomond, and on his way home crossed the south of Scotland. He spent a night at the Dumfries Arms Hotel in Cumnock on 29 June 1817. Next day he headed for Drumlanrig Castle, stopping for lunch at Sanquhar, where he was inspired to write a short verse 'To His Grace the Duke of Buccleuch', detailing his recent itinerary:

From Ross, where the clouds on Benlomond are sleeping –
From Greenock, where the Clyde to the ocean is sweeping –
From Largs, where the Scotch gave the Northmen a drilling –
From Ardrossan, whose harbour cost many a shilling –

From Old Cumnock, where beds are as hard as a plank,
sir –
From a chop and green pease, and a chicken at Sanquhar,
This eve, please the Fates, at Drumlanrig we anchor.

The Dumfries Arms was opened for coaching traffic on 25 March 1717, when it was known as the New, or Heid, Inn (because it was the first inn outside the old part of the town). It was named the Dumfries Arms, after the local landowners, Earls of Dumfries, in 1840. Among other notables who stayed there was, inevitably, Robert Burns.

The Cafe Royal in Edinburgh's West Register Street is a fairly modern restaurant, but the building incorporates the old Ambrose's Tavern: the setting for 'Christopher North's' series of dialogues in *Blackwood's Magazine*, 'Noctes Ambrosianae', which invoked Scott, Hogg and other major literary figures from the early nineteenth century. Also in Edinburgh, Jenny Ha's Tavern and Ale House stands off the

Dumfries Arms Hotel, Cumnock

Canongate, at Callender's Entry, near Whitefoord House. Established in the eighteenth century as Jenny Ha's Change House, this hostelry was frequented by the poets Allan Ramsay and John Gay.

The Howgate Inn, probably dating from around 1794, stood beside the A6094 just south of Penicuik until it was destroyed by fire in 1994. This was the home of the fictional Howgate Carrier in Dr John Brown's *Rab and His Friends* (1859). It was also at one time the home of a small brewery, 'the strong ale [enjoying] a high reputation locally and [being] served in elegant conical stemmed glasses'. At the end of the eighteenth century, when Walter Scott and three others stayed during a fishing trip in the Pentlands in their student days, the innkeeper was Margaret Dodds; Scott later used the name Meg Dodds for the hostess of the Cleikum Inn in *St Ronan's Well* (1823), though the character was based on another.

Another old Lothian hostelry is the Ninemileburn Inn, also known as Habbie's Howe Hotel, located on the south side of the Pentland Hills and nine miles from Edinburgh on the A702. (If you measure it you will find the distance from the Castle to the inn seems to be in excess of eleven miles, but we must remember that this inn was named when the 'lang Scotch miles' were still in use.) A board over the doorway advises the traveller with time on his hands how best to spend it:

> Gae farrer down the burn taes Habbie's Howe,
> Whaur a' the sweets o' summer grow,
> And when yer tired o' prattlin' 'side the rill,
> Return to Nine Mile Burn, an' tak' a gill.

Habbie's Howe was associated with Allan Ramsay's play *The Gentle Shepherd*, written in 1725, and the inn sign has two quotations from his works. In nearby Carlops is the Allan Ramsay Inn, a two-storey building dating from 1792, which has a portrait of Ramsay over the doorway.

The Hawes Inn in Queensferry (formerly known as New-halls Inn and Postinghouse) has associations with both Sir Walter Scott and Robert Louis Stevenson. It is said to stand on the site of a hospice erected by Queen Margaret for pilgrims en route to Dunfermline Abbey or St Andrews Cathedral, and across the road is the Hawes Pier from where they would have sailed to North Queensferry. The oldest part of the inn has two corbie-stepped gables facing the street and a public clock over the entrance doorway. This part, its walls whitewashed and the window-openings picked out in black in the old Scots manner, probably dates from 1683. The inn was extended to the west in the early nineteenth century, and to the east in 1893.

Scott used the Hawes Inn as the place where Jonathon Oldbuck and William Lovel stayed in *The Antiquary* (1816), in which it is described as 'a very decent sort of place' whose landlord was 'fat, gouty, pursy ... with that mixture of familiarity and respect which the Scotch innkeepers of the old school used to assume towards their more valued customers'. Stevenson visited regularly and stayed for a time in Room 13, where he began writing *Kidnapped* (1886). The novel begins at the inn, where the hero, David Balfour, is kidnapped by Captain Hoseason and Ebenezer Balfour and taken across the Forth from the pier that is visible from the bedroom where Stevenson wrote. Paintings of characters from his novel adorn the exterior of the inn. Stevenson had had a mind to involve the Hawes in a novel for some time, for in his letters he says:

> There it stands, apart from the town, beside the pier, in a climate of its own, half inland, half marine – in front the ferry bubbling with the tide and the guardship swinging her anchor; behind, the old garden with the trees. Americans seek it already for the sake of Lovel and Oldbuck, who dined there in *The Antiquary*. But you need not tell me – that is not all, there is some story, unrecorded or not yet complete, which must express the meaning of that inn more fully.

Also associated with Stevenson is the Cramond Inn, in the village of the same name to the west of (and now virtually part of) Edinburgh. The oldest part of the inn dates from 1670 – additions were made in 1887 and 1977 – and today it is a typically Scottish-style inn, white painted with black window and door surrounds. The roof is pantiled in the east-coast fashion, and there is a distinctive Venetian window at first floor level. It was at this inn that Robert Louis Stevenson once carved his initials on a table.

At Bridge of Allan, north of Stirling, stand two hotels of note, the Queens Hotel and the Royal Hotel, dating from the eighteenth and mid-nineteenth centuries respectively. These were popular when Bridge of Allan was a spa town. Robert Louis Stevenson spent nights in each of these hotels on a number of occasions, for he often came to Bridge of Allan as a child and as a young man. A plaque in the Royal Hotel claims that Stevenson stayed there in 1867, but this has been proved to be an incorrect date. However, Charles Dickens did spend a night there in 1867, while travelling round Britain giving public readings from his books.

Stirling is an ancient town spreading around its rock-built castle. In King Street the Golden Lion Hotel, erected in 1786 as a coaching inn, is distinguished by its pedimented bay. On 26 August 1787, when it was visited by Robert Burns and Willie Nicol on their way north to tour the Highlands, it was called James Wingate's Inn (it was later called Gibb's Red Lion Hotel). The poet slept in a room on the second floor at the north-east corner, where he scratched on a window-pane what are known as the 'Stirling Lines':

> Here Stewarts once in glory reign'd,
> And laws for Scotland's weal ordained:
> But now unroofed their palace stands,
> Their sceptre falled to other hands;
> Fallen indeed, and to the earth,
> When grovelling reptiles take their birth;

The injured Stewart line is gone,
A race outlandish fills their throne;
An idiot race, to honour lost –
Who knows them best, despise them most.

(These lines were to haunt Burns for many years afterwards.
Because of this slur on the Hanoverian royal house he was
often questioned about his beliefs, especially when working
with the excise later in life.) Later guests at the Golden Lion
included William and Dorothy Wordsworth, who spent the
night there in 1803, and Queen Victoria and Prince Albert,
guests in 1893, who are recorded as being most impressed.

The Kenmore Inn, in Kenmore village at the foot of Loch
Tay, lays claim to be one of the oldest public houses in
Scotland. It was opened in 1572, when Sir Colin Campbell
granted the first lease of the building to his servant Hew Hay
and his spouse on 2 November, and rebuilt in the 1760s. The
inn was visited by Burns, on his tour of the Highlands, on 29
August 1787. Over the chimney-piece on the wall of what is
now the Poet's Parlour he scribbled a three-verse poem (now
preserved under glass) that begins:

Admiring nature in her wildest grace.
These northern scenes with weary feet I trace;
O'er many a winding dale and painful steep,
Th' abodes of coveyed grouse and timid sheep,
My savage journey, curious, I view.
Till fam'd Breadalbane opens to my view.

R.L. Willis (a writer) visited Kenmore in 1799 and was
thrilled with his stay. He recorded that 'The cheapness of the
inn is wonderful. We had today for dinner, fine fresh trout, a
shoulder of mutton, two fowls and bacon, hung beef, and
salmon salted, vegetables, cheese and an excellent bottle of
port; and the sum total was four shillings and twopence'.
Dorothy Wordsworth, too, stopped at Kenmore and noted in

her journal the 'very beautiful prospect' from the large bow window.

Burns also paid a visit to the Inver Inn at the village of the same name, just outside Dunkeld on the north bank of the River Tay. Here he met the famous Scots fiddler and composer Neil (or Niel) Gow (1727–1807), who composed many of the tunes used for Burns's songs. The inn was one of the King's Houses established originally by the government at the same time as the military roads and was an important resting place for travellers because – before 1808, when Thomas Telford built a bridge – the Tay had to be crossed here by one of two small ferries. According to tradition, when the weather was misty a cow would swim in front of the boat to show the way! Another visitor who came to the inn to listen to Neil Gow was Elizabeth Grant of Rothiemurchus. In her *Memoirs of a Highland Lady* she wrote that 'old Niel Gow [was] sent for to play to us at the inn at Inver', and of another visit, en route north from Edinburgh, she recalled:

> The little inn at Inver was done up, a fine hotel where the civilest of Landlords reigned, close to the bridge, received all travellers; and Neil Gow was dead, the last of our bards – no one again will ever play Scotch musick as he did. His sons in the quick measures were perhaps his equals, they gave force and spirit and fine expression to Strathspeys and reels, but they never gave the slow, the tender airs with the real feeling of their beauty that their father had.

The Inver Inn no longer operates as a public house, for it has been converted into housing.

On his way back south, Burns stopped at the Gardenstone Arms Hotel in Laurencekirk, a small town between Brechin and Stonehaven, and a plaque commemorating his visit was unveiled here in 1972. Earlier visitors included Johnson and Boswell, who stayed en route to the Islands on 21 August 1773. The hotel was built by Lord Gardenstone, the local laird, as a place of rest for travellers and an asset to the local community, and it contained a small museum in which the Laurencekirk Public Library was housed. Boswell wrote in his *Journal of a Tour to the Hebrides* 'Dr Johnson insisted on stopping at the inn, as I told him that Lord Gardenston had furnished it with a collection of books, that travellers might have entertainment for the mind, as well as the body. He praised the design, but wished there had been more books, and those better chosen'.

This hotel was originally named the Boar's Head Inn, and its first landlord was William Cruikshank in the 1770s. He was noted in the Mearns for his skill as a bleeder, or person who could treat ailments. People would travel miles in the hope of a cure from him. His wife was noted for a similar ability to effect cures by natural means, and a picture of her by the Dutch artist Brich depicts her seated at a table, on which are scissors, hour-glass, phials and other objects. By her side is a girl in pain, whose finger Mrs Cruikshank is studying; another girl looks on, and the inn cat lies at the landlady's feet. An old poem popular in the area commemorates her skills:

> The gratefull village bless'd her name,
> And all the country spoke her fame,
> For she of every herb and flower,
> Had learnt the wonder-working power,
> And knew by secret art to drain,
> The juice that gives relief to pain,
> In ready order rang'd around,
> The balm that soothes the throbbing wound;
> Salves, cordials, balsams, – all were there,
> As various ills required her care.

Amongst those who stayed at the Gardenstone Arms was George Colman (1762–1836), the English dramatist, who stayed several times in 1782, when travelling back and forth to King's College in Aberdeen. In the hotel's album he wrote a few lines of doggerel that included the words:

> [I] deposited upon a profane altar [my] virgin offering to the Muse.

The lines offended the locals, one of whom wrote in riposte:

> I like thy wit; but, could I see thy face,
> I'd claw it well for Scotia's vile disgrace.

Colman read the retort on his next visit and added a further couplet:

> Is, then, a Scotchman such a clawing elf?
> I thought he scratched no creature but himself!

On 21 June 1819 Laurencekirk Town Council convened for a meeting at the Gardenstone Arms in a room subsequently known as the Council Room. The council seems to have moved round the inns of the town in turn, for four others also hosted their meetings.

In the Argyll village of Inveraray are two notable old inns. The Great Inn, which faces the castle of Inveraray, home of the Dukes of Argyll, was erected in 1750 by the third Duke, and for many years was known as the Argyll Head, then Argyll Arms Hotel. The architects responsible were John and Robert Adam, who also worked at the castle. The inn took five years to build, because most of the tradesmen were employed in building the castle, and work on the inn perhaps only went ahead when the castle work was held up. It cost £1,400 to build, entirely paid for by the Duke, and required 6,000 feet of timber to be imported from Frederikstad in Norway and 218,000 slates from Easdale.

Samuel Johnson and James Boswell stayed at this inn on their way home from the Hebrides in 1773, and it was here that Johnson tasted whisky for the first time. Boswell describes it as an 'excellent inn'; Johnson called it 'not only commodious but magnificent', and was inspired to mark the occasion by composing a 'Meditation of a Pudding'. Burns called at the Argyll Arms in 1787, but found the service not to his liking (it is said that they were too busy preparing for the arrival of the Duke of Argyll and his family). The bard is said to have scrawled the following lines on a window-pane in anger:

> There's naething here but Hielan' pride,
> An' Hieland scab, an' hunger;
> If Providence has sent me here,
> 'Twere surely in his anger.

The window no longer exists (indeed it may never have existed), but in a publication of 1799, it was stated that Burns wrote 'on a pane of glass in a Highland Inn':

> Highland Pride, Highland Scab, Highland hunger.
> If God Almighty sent me here, 'twas surely in his anger.

The Wordsworths stayed at the inn in 1803, Dorothy noting that it was 'over rich in waiters and large rooms to be exactly to our taste, though quite in harmony with the neighbour-hood'. Others who put up at the Great Inn included Robert Heron (author of *Journey Through the Western Counties of Scotland in Autumn of 1792*) and Sir John Stoddart (author of *Remarks on Local Scenery and Manners in Scotland* (1801)).

The other old inn at Inveraray is the George Hotel in Front Street, which was founded in 1720, although the present building was not erected until 1778. When the old village of Inveraray was cleared away (between 1746 and 1785) from the immediate surroundings of the castle, the inhabitants used the George Hotel as a place of worship for a time (the

present church dates from 1800–1805). In 1878 Lord
Malcolm of Poltalloch stayed at the George when he
contended against Lord Colin Campbell for the Argyll
parliamentary seat. Argyll was Campbell country, and it was
a brave man who came to Inveraray at this time; when the
election result was announced Malcolm had, not unexpec-
tedly, come second. According to an old guide-book to the
town, 'in the general enthusiasm which followed, Poltalloch
and his few loyal supporters suffered somewhat both in
dignity and property. When Lord Malcolm drove away from
the 'George', it was amid a thunder of ironical applause, and
the windows of both hotel and carriage, as well as houses of
supporters resident in the Square, suffered under a shower of
missiles'.

When Burns was on his tour of Argyll he visited Tarbet on
the way home – although he stayed at an older inn than the
present large Tarbet Hotel, standing at the road junction,
which was erected in the Victorian period. He is said to have
composed a poem (now lost) in honour of the inn-keeper's
daughter, a Miss MacLauchlan. William Wordsworth
conceived the idea for his poem 'Highland Lass' when he and
his sister spent a night at the Strathyre Inn in Perthshire (now
simply called The Inn) in 1803. They also stayed at the Luib
Inn in Glen Dochart (then known as Tynluib, or Tigh an
Luib); William must have liked the inn well enough, for he
stayed there again in 1814 with his wife and sister-in-law.
This inn has been converted into a farmhouse.

Professor John Stuart Blackie stayed ten nights at the
Columba Inn on the island of Iona while revising his *Lays of
the Highlands and Islands* before publication in 1871; he also
spent some time wandering over the island, which resulted in
a series of sonnets. The Columba Inn was originally the Free
Church Manse, but it had been converted into a hotel by the
Duke of Argyll and leased to Mary Ritchie in 1868.

At the village of Cruden Bay, eight miles south of
Peterhead, stands the Kilmarnock Arms, a two-storey

building adorned with a coat of arms and named after the fourth Earl of Kilmarnock, a Jacobite who was beheaded in 1746. In 1894 the author Bram Stoker spent a number of nights here on holiday. In his journal he wrote, 'When first I saw the place I fell in love with it. Had it been possible, I should have spent my summer there in a house of my own, but the want of any place in which to live forbade such an opportunity. So I stayed in the little hotel, the Kilmarnock Arms', and the inn's visitors' book contains his comment: 'Delighted with everything and everybody and hope to come again'. The village of Cruden Bay was the inspiration for *The Watter's Mou'* (1894), a tale about smuggling. *Crooken Sands* and *The Mystery of the Sea* (1902) followed, both set in the locality. Stoker's best-known work, *Dracula* was not to appear until 1897, by which time he had acquired a holiday cottage at Whinnyfold, a tiny hamlet at the other end of the two-mile-long Bay of Cruden; Dracula's castle was based on the castle of Slains, which still stands in ruins nearby. James Cruikshank, the proprietor of the Kilmarnock Arms when Stoker stayed there, and his daughter Bella asked Stoker where he got his weird ideas from. He told them they came to him, 'walking along the cliffs, walking along the sands of Cruden'.

Burns was known for his habit of etching verses or his name on panes of glass wherever he went, but the author of *Peter Pan* and *The Admirable Crichton* was known to do the same. J.M. Barrie's initials are etched on the window of the dining room at the Harris Hotel, at Tarbert on the island of Harris. He visited in 1912, and was joined by Anthony Hope (Hawkins), author of *The Prisoner of Zenda* and E.V. Lucas, the essayist, biographer and novelist. They visited Barrie at Amhuinnsuidhe Castle, which he had rented from Sir Samuel Scott in order to give the orphaned Llewellyn Davies boys a holiday. It was on Harris that Barrie pulled together the idea for *Mary Rose*, a play based on an old Scottish ballad called 'Bonny Kilmeny', though he did not write it until some years later. One of the characters in the play – the ghillie, a Highlander by the name of Cameron – was based on the son of the owners of the Harris Hotel, David Cameron, who had ghillied for Barrie during his stay on the island.

Another writer whose name is etched on a window is John Keats. Travelling round the Highlands in 1818, with Armitage Brown, he stopped at the Cairndow Stagecoach Inn in the village of Cairndow, at the foot of Glen Kinglas, and bathed in Loch Fyne. Two-and-a-half storeys in height, this is a typically Scots change-house, today whitewashed and with blue window-openings. Inside is preserved a pane of glass bearing Keats's name and a letter in which, having forgotten the name of the place, he refers to 'Cairn-something'. Keats and Brown had walked thirteen miles to Cairndow from Arrochar across the wild Rest and be Thankful pass (Keats was disappointed to find that the Rest and be Thankful was not an inn, as he had thought). Keats was ill at the time and died three years later.

Earlier visitors to this inn were the ubiquitous Wordsworths. They spent the night of 29 August 1803 here, but, on waking at seven 'were completely out of patience' because none of the staff was awake. Nevertheless, they recorded with gratitude that they had breakfasted on herrings freshly caught in Loch Fyne. Dorothy wrote:

> We were ... well received and sat down in a neat parlour with a good fire. Breakfasted before our departure and ate herring fresh from the water, at our landlord's earnest recommendation. Cairndow is a single house by the side of the loch, I believe, resorted to by gentlemen in the fishing season; it is a pleasant place for such a purpose.

Queen Victoria did not spend the night at the Cairndow Inn, but on 29 September 1875 her entourage stopped to change horses there. She recorded the event in her journal:

Changed horses at a small inn called Cairndow where the dear little Campbell children are staying, and who were at the windows – such lovely children! There were a few people collected, and the harness as well as the horses had to be changed, and a pair of leaders put on to pull us up the long steep ascent in Glen Kinglas.

6   Soldiers' Sorties

The late seventeenth century was a time of religious struggle in Scotland, particularly in the south-west. King Charles II wished to impose Episcopacy on the Scots, to bring the country into line with England, but this was seen by Presbyterians as every bit as unwelcome as Roman Catholicism. Many ministers were thrown out of their churches, and thousands of individuals refused to swear allegiance to the king before God; as a result, they were forced to hide in the hills and moors, and government soldiers were sent to search them out and kill them if need be. A number of 'Covenants' were drawn up and signed by thousands of Scots. One of them was renewed at an inn in Edinburgh's Old Town, the Cross Keys, which stood in an alley now known as Covenant Close.

One of the most notorious persecutors of the Covenanters, as these hill-men were known, was John Graham of Claverhouse (c. 1649–89), known at this time as 'Bloody Clavers', and later as 'Bonnie Dundee'. Holding the King's commission to suppress the religious rebels of south-west Scotland, he led a group of soldiers through the Southern Uplands, searching out those who had signed the Solemn League and Covenant and putting them to death. He made the Black Bull Inn at Moffat his headquarters during the treacherous period known as the 'Killing Times', (1683–5) and is said to have built the stables (now the Railway Bar)

Black Bull Inn, Moffat

adjoining the inn. This inn, founded in 1568, was one of the oldest buildings in Moffat and later became a major change-house on the route from Edinburgh to the south. Its accommodation was not always of the best, however, for at the time when it was run by Provost Johnston its beds were described (by Joseph Taylor in *A Journey to Edenborough in Scotland*, 1705) as unfit to sleep in.

A regular user of the Black Bull in later years was Robert Burns, who on one occasion inscribed on one of its windows, using a diamond stylus, his 'Epigram on Miss Davies (On Being Asked Why She Had Been Formed So Little and Mrs. A—— So Big)'.

> Ask why God made the gem so small, and why so huge
>   the granite,
> Because God meant mankind should set the higher value
>   on it.

This window was removed from the inn and is believed to have been presented to the Tsar of Russia; the locals claim that it is currently stored in a museum in Moscow! A replica of the window was unveiled at the inn on 17 July 1996 by Murdo Morrison, president of the Burns Federation. Burns's drinking song 'Willie Brew'd a Peck o' Maut' was said to have been composed at the Black Bull.

Another inn that has associations with both Covenanting and with Burns is the Loudoun Arms at Newmilns in Ayrshire. The building has thick stone walls, pedimented windows at eaves level and a corbie-stepped gable, and behind it stands the old tower or castle of Newmilns (recently restored), which dates from the sixteenth century. In April 1685 it was used as a prison for a group of Covenanters caught holding a prayer meeting, or conventicle, at a nearby farm. They were taken to the keep and were locked up for the night, but a number of locals attacked the building and managed to set them free. In the melee John Law was killed and buried where he fell, and a memorial on an adjacent wall commemorates him:

> Cause I Christ's Prisoners reliev'd,
> I of my life was soon beriev'd.
> By cruel Enemies with rage,
> In that rencounter did engage.
> The Martyr's honour & his Crown,
> Bestow'd on me O high Renown,
> That I Should not only believe,
> But for Christ's cause my life should give.

Robert Burns visited the Loudoun Arms on 27 March 1786, when he was installed as an Honorary Member of Masonic Lodge No. 51, Loudoun Kilwinning Newmilns. According the lodge's minutes, he was introduced by Gavin Hamilton of Mauchline, Right Worshipful Master, and admitted 'much to the satisfaction of the Lodge'.

One of the most noted Covenanting martyrs was Richard Cameron, who was born at Falkland in Fife in 1648 and killed at the Battle of Airds Moss in Ayrshire on 22 July 1680. His birthplace in Falkland survives, and two doors along is an old inn which has been named the Covenanter

Hotel. One of its windows has a marriage lintel inscribed with the date 1771, but the building is believed to be much older. During the early 1800s there was an auction here at which virtually everything apart from the walls and roof was sold; bids were accepted for the doors, windows, glass and panelling! In more recent times the inn has welcomed some notable guests, including Johnny Cash, Ian Paisley, Andy Williams and numerous politicians. Whether or not they experienced the inn's ghost is not recorded. A female figure is said to appear in some of the bedrooms, and on odd occasions things have been known to 'fly' across the room. Some reckon that the spirit is that of Mary, Queen of Scots, who spent some of her happiest times at nearby Falkland Palace.

The Sun Inn at Douglas, south of Lanark, was built in 1621 and has now been converted into a private house with the assistance of the National Trust for Scotland. It was here the severed head and hands of Richard Cameron were brought after being hacked from his corpse at Airds Moss (the room in which they lay was known as the Stane Room, from its slabbed floor); a number of other Covenanters were held prisoner here, including the commander at the battle, David Hackston of Rathillet. It was in Douglas that the Cameronian regiment was raised, named in honour of the martyr, and it was here in 1968 it was disbanded. The building still has its old corbie-stepped gables and typical stair tower to the rear.

At Moniaive in the Dumfriesshire dales the George Hotel stands in the High Street, next to the bridge over the Cairn Water. This inn, which dates from 1624, is claimed to be one of the oldest in Scotland, and certainly the oldest in Dumfriesshire. Its undressed roof timbers support a slate roof done in the old Galloway manner, with slates diminishing in size as they near the ridge. There are original stone flagstones in the bar, and the windows still have their original wooden lintels. Government soldiers hunting the Covenanters did not

George Hotel, Moniaive

use this inn as a base, but the Covenanters themselves found it a useful hiding place, and a place of concealment used in the years of struggle still survives in the building. The Covenanter's secret hole is half-way up the staircase at the rear, where a small modern doorway (the original was probably hidden by a hanging tapestry or picture) gives access to a space between the ground-floor ceiling and the roof that could accommodate two men at a pinch. A spy-hole that used to allow them to look down Glen Cairn no longer exists.

Another interesting relic in the George is the Tramp's Hole: a small square hole in the fireplace lintel where the villagers left their odd change for the benefit of men of the road. If there was enough in the hole, they could get a drink or meal at the inn. Small change is still collected in it, but, as the last tramp left the district a few years ago, this is now given to charity. During recent renovation work at the inn, a small child's leather shoe, in excellent condition, was found beneath the floorboards of the first-floor room; it was an old custom to build a small shoe into buildings to ensure good luck. Across the road is a small building, now a garage, that used to be the inn stables. At one time the George was used as the local police station.

A number of 'lost' inns had associations with Covenanters. One of them, the Blue Tower Inn, stood in what is now known as Tower Street in Cumnock. This was one of the oldest buildings in the burgh, and some of the soldiers who were policing the south-west stayed here whilst escorting a prisoner to Edinburgh. The next day, as they passed through the Bello Path east of Lugar, they were ambushed by the Covenanters, and their prisoner, the Rev. David Houston, was freed. One of the Covenanters, John MacGeachan, was injured in the affray and died a few weeks later; his grave is in a nearby field.

The first Jacobite rebellion took place in 1715. At that time a number of conspirators met in the Smugglers' Inn at Anstruther in Fife, where the Earl of Strathmore was staying, and planned to depose King George I in favour of James Stuart (the 'Old Pretender'), the son of James II, who had been overthrown in 1688. After the meeting the Earl went to Anstruther Cross, where he proclaimed the Pretender to be king. The pistols he carried that day and the wine drunk during the proceedings were, according to the burgh collector of the time, 'never paid for'. (In Anstruther's archives there also survives a letter from Bonnie Prince Charlie's secretary, James Murray of Broughton, thanking the townsfolk for quartering the Jacobite troops in the second rebellion of 1745.) The Smugglers was at one time known as the Commercial Inn.

In 1745 the Jacobite general Lord George Murray spent a night at the Black Bull Inn at Cumbernauld, during a march from Glasgow to Stirling. The building was originally a town house of the Wigtons of Cumbernauld, but was converted to an inn when the present Cumbernauld House was completed in 1731; it was also used as an overflow when there were too many visitors to accommodate at Cumbernauld House. In the later eighteenth and nineteenth centuries the inn was a top-class hostelry, but it was eventually demolished and a house erected on its site. For years afterwards the exact location was forgotten, and it was not until 1966, when excavations were being made for a new house, that the former inn's vaulted cellar was discovered; this had been filled with packed earth, which contained fragments of artefacts that confirmed the building's origins.

In Duddingston – now part of Edinburgh – there survives an inn that Bonnie Prince Charlie is said to have visited when he was lodged in the village (the house where he stayed also survives). The Sheep's Heid Inn at the Causeway must be one of the oldest inns in Scotland. It is claimed to date from 1360, and was rebuilt in 1670, but much of the present building was erected in the eighteenth century and extended in Edwardian times. Mary Queen of Scots is known to have paid a visit to the inn whilst travelling to Craigmillar Castle, and another royal visitor was her son King James VI (later James I of England), who was so impressed with the hostelry that around 1580 he gave the landlord a snuff-mull in the form of a ram's head. This remained on view at the inn until 1888 when it was unfortunately sold, and its current location is unknown. One historic relic still at the inn is a disc cast from the metal of the Tron Church bell which melted in the Great Fire of Edinburgh in November 1824; there is also a fine selection of ancient trophies, including a silver snuff-box, a large ram's head and a blue Bristol decanter. At the back of the inn is a rare skittle alley (the oldest in Scotland), and the skittle club that plays here has records going back to the eighteenth century. In the winter months the Sheep's Heid used to be frequented by curlers, Duddingston Loch being a popular location for the 'roaring game'. Among notable regulars to visit the inn in the nineteenth century were the lawyer-poet Henry Glassford Bell and publisher Dr Robert Chambers (1802–71).

When Bonnie Prince Charlie was staying at the Palace of Holyroodhouse in Edinburgh in 1745 his soldiers are said to have been put up at the White Horse Inn in the city's Canongate. At Crieff in Perthshire is the Drummond Arms Hotel in the main street; this was built on the site of an older inn of the same name at which the Young Pretender held a council of war on 3 February 1746 that was noted for its heated debate.

A number of inns that no longer survive were associated with Charles Edward Stuart. A large retail store now occupies the site of the Buck's Head Inn in Glasgow's Argyle Street, where he stayed at some time in the eighteenth century – and where in 1819 Robert Southey noted that 'large as this house is, they had no room with a fire when we arrived, cold and hungry, at ten o'clock on a wet morning'. The inn was demolished and a new building erected on the site in 1863. Before going to Glasgow, the Prince had visited Airdrie and lodged with his officers in the high street at 'Tibbie Tamson's Change House' – long-since gone, and its site forgotten. They are reputed to have drunk the village dry and failed to pay for their accommodation. Tibbie was later to remark, 'I would raither ha'e a chapman's groat than a prince's promise'.

At Glenfinnan, on the road to Mallaig from Fort William, stands that tall monument commemorating the raising of the Prince's standard there on 19 August 1745. At that time there were few houses in Glenfinnan, but there was an inn, believed to have been erected in 1658. Known variously as the Glenfinnan Inn and the Stage House, it has recently been renamed the Prince's House (some say that the Prince might just have taken a drink there!). According to *Cycle, Camp and Camera*, written in 1909 by E.E. Henderson and J. Walker, one of the windows facing the monument at that time bore the following lines:

Ah! where is the heart that no sorrow can feel,
As he wanders along by the banks of Loch Shiel?
To the sound of his pibroch these mountains did ring,
And this is the spot that gave Scotland her king;
'Twas here that the Standard of War was unfurled,
From the hills of the north, Highland vengeance was hurled,
And brave were the hearts that rushed down on the plain:
Say, Harp of the Highlands, ah! rushed they in vain?
But soft lies the turf of green France on his head,
And sweet is the sleep of the warrior's bed;
And true were the clansmen that gathered in might –
How kind now in peace, and how valiant in fight?

The inn later became a notable coaching halt and, in Victorian times, a popular rendezvous for stalking and fishing parties; the 1910 season's catch for Loch Shiel, on which the hotel had the fishing rights, was 1,555 sea trout, 22 salmon and 56 brown trout. According to *Scotland and the*

Glenfinnan Inn, Inverness-shire (now known as The Prince's House)

Scotch by Catherine Sinclair, written in 1840, the inn-keeper of the time was 'the tallest man in the Highlands, who measures six feet seven – or seven feet six – and is large in proportion'. The inn has been extended a couple of times, but the Gothic windows are still a notable feature. Here too, one may sometimes witness a ghost, for a Grey Lady and Bearded Highlander make rare appearances, but they seem not to be troublesome.

The inn at Glenfinnan played a part in saving the life of Malcolm MacAlpine (born 1877), son of Sir Robert MacAlpine, the founder of the building firm. Malcolm was working on the construction of a new railway (Fort William–Mallaig), when blasting sent a lump of rock flying for 1,200 feet. This landed on him, causing severe bleeding and internal injuries, and word was sent to his father in Glasgow that the boy was unlikely to survive. Sir Robert persuaded Professor MacEwen (later Sir William) to accompany him on a specially chartered train to Fort William, and the following afternoon they reached the scene of the accident, where the Professor performed an operation on site. They remained there for a few days, but Professor MacEwen stated that the only chance of saving the boy was to get him back to the hospital in Glasgow. The next day MacAlpine arranged for eight men to carry a stretcher over the hills to a loch, down which the boy was taken by boat. A ten-mile trek to Glenfinnan followed, but when the Stage House was reached the door was not wide enough for the stretcher – so a window was knocked out and the stretcher passed through. Next day the bearers carried the boy seven miles to a point where the railway lines were in place and taken down to Glasgow, where he made a full recovery.

The former inn at Dalnacardoch, west of Blair Atholl, was erected on the site of a wooden hut used by General Wade when building his Military Roads in the 1720s. This was later converted into an inn which was visited by Bonnie Prince Charlie on 30 August 1745. On the retreat after his ill-fated march to Derby he stayed at the inn again on 10 and 11 February 1746, two months before the Battle of Culloden. Colonel Thomas Thornton, the sporting writer (1757–1823) stayed here in 1786 and dined on 'Hodge Podge, Pudding, greens, trout and char, roast mutton, excellent; Second course bandered chickens, cold hams, snipes, Cheshire cheese – biscuits, wines, claret, good, port ditto, limes, Jamaica rum and incomparable porter from Claverts.' A later visitor was Queen Victoria who changed horses here on 9 October 1861 and noted in her journal:

> We had one very heavy shower after Loch Garry and before we came to Dalnacardoch Inn, thirteen miles from Dalwhinnie. The road goes beside the Garry. The country for a time became flatter; but was a good deal cultivated. At Dalnacardoch Inn there was a suspicion and expectation of our arrival. Four horses with smart postilions were in waiting; but, on General Grey's saying that this was *not* the party, but the one for whom only two horses had been ordered, a shabby pair of horses were put in; a shabby driver driving from the box (as throughout this journey), and off we started.

Later converted to a hunting lodge for the Dukes of Atholl, the inn has since become a ruin. It used to bear an old sign that read: *Hospitivm Hoc in Publicvm Commodivm, Georgivs III Rex Constrvi ivssit A.D. 1774. Rest a little while. Gabhaif fois car tamvill bhig.* A couple of miles away is the Wade Stone – a huge boulder, eight feet high and four feet wide, bearing the date 1729. General Wade placed a guinea on the top of it when he was in the area and was surprised to find it still there a year later.

One result of the first Jacobite uprising in 1715 was the building of a new road system over much of the Highlands. Garrisons were established at new barracks – at Fort William, Fort Augustus, Fort George, Bernera, Inversnaid, and Ruthven and elsewhere – in order to prevent any future uprising and to enforce the new laws of the land, particularly those on the wearing of tartan and illicit distilling. New 'military roads' were built over much of the Highlands to allow the soldiers to traverse the countryside with greater speed (though the Jacobites also used the roads to their advantage on many occasions).

The most famous name associated with the building of these roads is that of Major-General – subsequently Field Marshal – George Wade (1673–1748). A rhyming couplet meant that his name survived long after he had severed his connection with road construction, the work being continued by others, including General Caulfield. The rhyme goes:

> If you had seen these roads before they were made,
> You'd lift up your heart and bless General Wade.

Wade is known to have built 250 miles of road, including 42 bridges, between the years 1725 and 1738, when he was Commander-in-Chief in Scotland with the task of demili-tarizing the Highlands. He spent a number of nights based at the Weem Inn, in the village of the same name near Aberfeldy, in 1733, making it his headquarters for a time. This inn has a portrait of the general on its exterior and lies near the very fine Tay Bridge, construction of which Wade was overseeing at the time. The bridge, designed by the Scots architect William Adam of Maryburgh (father of James and Robert Adam) and completed in 1734, is still in constant use.

The Crook Inn stands in upper Tweeddale, seventeen miles north of Moffat and sixteen miles from Peebles. It is said to have been founded in 1604; though it has been considerably extended over the years, and its advertisements claim it to be 'Scotland's oldest licensed inn'. Sir Thomas Dick Lauder, writing in *Scottish Rivers* in 1807, described the inn as 'one of the coldest-looking, cheerless places of reception for travellers that we had ever chanced to behold'. It was not always so unwelcoming, however, for at the end of the seventeenth century, during the years when the struggle for the Covenant was at its fiercest, the landlady was a devout adherent and is said to have hid a persecuted Covenanter in the inn's peat-stack while soldiers were scouring the area for him. It is also recorded that a Covenanting minister (the Rev. James Thompson, minister of Tweedsmuir) was ordained at the inn on 5 September 1688.

Another landlady, Jeanie Hutchison, was well-known in the valley in the late eighteenth century as 'Jeanie o' the Crook'. A song of this name – written by local poet, Rev. Hamilton Paul, minister at Broughton – is sung to the tune 'Jock o' Hazeldean'. Jean is buried at the kirkyard of Tweedsmuir with the epithet, 'Jeanie o' the Crook', inscribed on her headstone.

An earlier tale takes us back to 1621. In that year Sir Patrick Porteous of Hawkshaw was being taken to Edinburgh to be tried for debt. At 'Cruik of Twedell' he and his escort stopped to break the journey overnight. The inn-keeper, James Geddes let word slip that Porteous was being held there, and a number of neighbours arrived and rescued Porteous, preventing his trial.

In the eighteenth century the landlord was a staunch Jacobite who was out with Bonnie Prince Charlie. He was captured at the battle of Culloden in 1746 and taken south towards Carlisle where he was expected to be put on trial. The route taken by the escort party passed by his own inn, and, this being countryside he knew well, the prisoner made plans for his escape. As the entourage continued southward, over the highest point of the route at Tweedshaws, he made his bid for freedom by lunging over the edge of the Devil's Beef Tub, a great corrie at the head of Annandale. Since the sides of this hollow are extremely steep, the soldiers reckoned that he would not survive the fall and continued on their way. The landlord did survive, however, and made his way back to the Crook Inn, where he remained hidden until the aftermath of Culloden had receded. This tale was used by Sir Walter

Scott in his novel *Redgauntlet*.

Though it is recorded that he far preferred a hostelry known as The Bield, nearer Tweedsmuir, Robert Burns also visited the Crook Inn on his journeys from Dumfries to Edinburgh. It is said that his poem 'Willie Wastle' was written in the kitchen of the Crook, 'the spot ca'd Linkumdoddie' being just over a mile to the north. Many other notables have put up at the Crook over the centuries. John Wilson (Christopher North) and James Hogg, the writers, both stayed there, and Lord Cockburn used the inn as a stop-over whilst on circuit. Sir Walter Scott spent a night at the inn in 1797 when heading south for the Lake District (he is thought to have used its name as the basis of the 'Cleikum Inn' in *St Ronan's Well*). Other visitors were Professors John Veitch, John Campbell Shairp and John Blackie, Dr John Brown, Alexander Russell and Andrew Lang. The *Strange Adventures of a Phaeton* (1872) by William Black describes a night at the Crook in the closing chapters.

The Crook Inn was closed at the beginning of the twentieth century, but later converted and reopened, much to the relief of weary and thirsty travellers. One of its fireplaces has a highly distinctive arched overmantel, made (it is said) by using an old cartwheel to support the stones until the mortar had set and then setting the cartwheel alight to leave the finished arch standing. It was at the Crook the Scottish Mountaineering Club was founded in 1891 – after the first meeting the members climbed Broad Law (2,756 feet), east of the inn. Today the club is noted for its authoritative guidebooks and for publishing *Munro's Tables*.

Another tale associated with the inn is reported in the *Peebleshire Advertiser* for 3 June 1831. At the time the roads from the Crook to Edinburgh were so bad that a visitor at the inn bet the driver of the mail coach that, given an hour's start, he would walk to Edinburgh and arrive there before him. The walker set off on the 36-mile journey, followed by the mail coach, and arrived at the depot in Edinburgh just as the coachman was loosening off his horse. Ten years later the *New Statistical Account* noted that the road was now in excellent repair.

A few other inns have associations with the Jacobite rising. One of the main battles in the first rebellion took place at Sheriffmuir, east of Dunblane, on 13 November 1715. The battle's indecisive outcome was encapsulated in an ironic verse:

> There's some say that we wan,
> And some say that they wan,
> And some say that nane wan at a', man;
> But ae thing I'm sure,
> That at Sheriffmuir,
> A battle there was that I saw man.
> And we ran and they ran, and they ran and we ran,
> And we ran, and they ran awa' man.

The Sheriffmuir Inn had only been open a few months when the battle took place, but soon it attracted many visitors who were keen to see the battlefield.

The Salutation Hotel in Perth's South Street is said to be the oldest established hotel in Scotland and, according to a plaque on the wall, was founded in 1699. The plaque goes on to quote *Chambers's Journal* of 1 May 1911, which told of the life of Colonel Bower of Kingaldrum in Angus (Forfarshire on the plaque). Colonel Bower was put on trial at York, charged with being a Jacobite. Yet, 'the only charge that could be brought against him was that he had worn a white cockade in his bonnet and had been seen shaking hands with Prince Charles Edward at the Salutation Inn in Perth'. The hotel is distinguished by its Georgian façade, with pilasters and huge fanlight window, as well as the alcove figures of kilted highlanders.

Bonnie Prince Charlie arrived at Perth on 4 September

Salutation Hotel, Perth

1745 and successfully took the town: the first he took in Scotland. He had with him 2,400 supporters and at the Cross he proclaimed his father King, as James VIII, and himself Regent. He stayed for four nights, collecting funds (or taxes) from the townspeople and from folk as far away as Dundee, and then continued his march towards Edinburgh. Charles is said to have stayed at the Salutation on his visit to Perth. Although some claim that he is more likely to have stayed at Lord Stormont's house in the High Street, the room at the Salutation in which he is supposed to have slept (number 120) is still pointed out.

The Broadford Hotel on the Island of Skye has a unique connection with Bonnie Prince Charlie. The Young Pretender hid on the island for a few days in 1746, after his defeat at Culloden, and was put up by various people on the island. Whether or not one of them was the landlord of the Broadford Inn, a Mackinnon, is not known, but the prince must have felt that he owed him some special debt, for on his departure he left him a copy of a secret recipe for a whisky liqueur. It is called Drambuie, from the Gaelic *Dram Buidheach*, meaning 'the drink that satisfies'; the recipe remains a secret in the same family, which now owns the Drambuie Liqueur Company. Its bottle labels carry the motto *Cuimhnich an tabhartas Prionnsa* ('remember the gift of the Prince'). Also on Skye is the Royal Hotel in Bank Street, Portree. This was erected on the site of a much older hostelry, known as MacNab's Inn, in which Bonnie Prince Charlie parted from Flora MacDonald on 1 July 1746. In 1773, the ubiquitous Boswell and Johnson arrived here to dine after a visit to the island of Raasay. They then travelled to Kingsburgh, where they met Flora MacDonald herself, 'a little woman, of a mild and genteel appearance, mighty soft and well-bred'.

The County Hotel in Dumfries (which no longer survives, its site being occupied by shops) also had associations with Prince Charles. It was originally known as the Blue Bell Inn; the prince used this building in the High Street as his headquarters on his march south towards Derby. The room he occupied was long after known as the Bonnie Prince Charlie Room and was reputedly haunted by his ghost. In 1798 the inn was leased by Jane Williamson (née Young), a niece of John Paul Jones, at which time it was renamed the Commercial Hotel. It later became the County, but was demolished in the 1980s.

* * *

Rob Roy MacGregor (1671–1734) is known as a Highland freebooter and cattle-reiver, something of a Scottish Robin Hood. The truth is slightly less romantic, for he was a much maligned man, forced from his house in midwinter and persecuted by neighbouring outlaws. Sir Walter Scott told his story in the highly successful novel *Rob Roy* (1818), relating how Rob Roy was beaten up with a 'poker' (really a plough coulter) by the Glasgow bailie Nicol Jarvie at an inn at Aberfoyle in Perthshire. This former inn has in recent years been restored, the thatched roof relaid and the wall rebuilt. Known as Jean MacAlpine's Inn in the seventeenth century, the building stands at Milton a mile west of Aberfoyle and probably originally dates from 1600.

In 1829 the Duke of Montrose erected a replacement inn, the Bailie Nicol Jarvie Hotel, on a site slightly further to the east of the original; there the coulter used by the Bailie was preserved until the hotel was converted into flats in 1996. Another inn associated with Nicol Jarvie is the Carbeth Inn, four miles north of Bearsden. According to Scott, it was here the Bailie and his companions stopped for food. The inn was little more than 'a miserable ale-house' but the travellers were well fed on a meal of game washed down with 'good brandy'. The present inn dates from 1816.

Rob Roy MacGregor was at one time held in gaol in the village of Logierait. The former gaol, which (erected around 1730) is now converted into the Logierait Inn, and the Regality Courthouse and cell are still intact within the building. Adjoining the inn is the hanging tree, where some prisoners met their end. It is thought that the last person to be executed here was one Donald Dubh (Black Donald), supposedly for sheep-stealing.

In 1795 a barracks was established in the east end of Glasgow, between what are now Barrack and Hunter streets. Here many Highland soldiers were billeted, and it is said that their favourite local hostelry was the inn at 328 Gallowgate which came to be known as Hielan' Jessie's. This has now been replaced by a new pub, known as Hielan Jessie, at 374 Gallowgate in a building dating from 1771 and restored in recent years. The barracks were closed in the 1870s, but the inn remained a popular hostelry long afterwards.

The old inn at Bellanoch has a story linking it not with soldiers but with the police. Bellanoch is a little clachan by the side of the Crinan Canal at the head of Loch Crinan. During the Great Famine of 1848 the police arrested five men who had been evicted from their crofts and who were causing trouble in the neighbourhood. They were taken under escort to the inn where they were held, but two hundred others marched to the inn, attacked the police and forcibly freed their friends.

The Second World War tended not to affect Scottish inns a great deal, though there are a few which have some connections. The Bridgend House Hotel at Callander dates from the eighteenth or, (some say) the seventeenth century. Its present external decoration of mock-Tudor timbers is the result of repairs after a Spitfire crashed into part of the building causing considerable damage. The ghosts which are said to haunt the inn don't date from the 1940s, however. Part of the inn was built over an old public path that led to The Meadows, and since then the spirits of various people have been seen walking through the inn's walls and rooms, following the ancient route.

At the southern end of Inveraray the Loch Fyne Hotel, formerly a small country house, achieved great importance in the Second World War, when it was the combined operations headquarters for the whole of the west coast of Scotland. The area around Inveraray had a number of hutted camps (later used to house Polish soldiers; many of whom decided to settle locally) where half a million troops trained before the Normandy landings. Winston Churchill paid a visit to the hotel in 1941, to inspect the naval and military units based in the area, and congratulated the locals for their patience and support for the war effort. The story of combined operations in the area is told in detail in an exhibition at Cherry Park in the grounds of Inveraray Castle.

Another Argyll hostelry with military connections is the Creggans Inn at Strachur on the south shore of Loch Fyne. Although not particularly old (it was built in 1910), it stands on the site of a much older coaching inn – even before coaches took to the roads there was an inn here when Mary Queen of Scots crossed the loch and landed at the little headland at Creggans. The inn used to be owned by the war hero Sir Fitzroy Maclean (1911–96), commander of the British military mission to the Yugoslav partisans during the Second World War and a founder-member of the SAS (some say he was the model for Ian Fleming's James Bond). He wrote extensively on his experiences. His widow is also a writer, though her speciality is books on cooking, and their son, Charles Maclean, writes books on Scottish subjects. The inn has attracted many notable guests over the years, from Roger Moore and Michael Caine to Joanna Lumley and Magnus Magnusson.

7   Tales to Tell

Many old inns have tales and legends associated with them – stories that have been handed down over the years by the landlords and regulars. A number of these can be regarded as pure fiction, but there are many that have some basis of fact behind them and can be regarded as true. The reader may decide which of the following tales fall into which category.

There are numerous haunted inns in Scotland. At Crocketford, on the main road from Dumfries to Castle Douglas, stands the Galloway Arms Hotel, which dates back to 1856. It was not always an inn, for it owes its origin to the Buchanites, a religious sect which was founded by Elizabeth Buchan (1738–91). Born in Banffshire, Buchan moved to Irvine in Ayrshire, where she persuaded the minister of the Relief Church that she had heavenly powers, claiming to be the woman referred to in Revelations 12. A group of her followers formed the Buchanites in 1784, but they were subsequently expelled from Irvine and, after travelling round the south-west, settled at Closeburn in Dumfriesshire and at Crocketford, where their former convent is now the Galloway Arms. According to a number of regulars at the bar, the hotel is haunted by Buchan herself, who appears at irregular intervals.

There is another apparition in the Craighead Inn at Cumnock. This is an old stone building that has recently been restored, but it was probably built in 1722, when a lease drawn up for the premises stipulated an annual rent of £21, plus two hens and two loads of coal! The attic rooms of the inn are said to be haunted by a spirit nicknamed 'Marvin' by the regulars. He seems to have appeared only a few times in recent years; at one time a man was sponsored to spend a full night alone in one of these bedrooms, which he managed to complete.

Just west of Larkhall, the Applebank Inn sits by the Millheugh Bridge across the Avon Water. The inn is fairly old, the earliest known reference to it being from 1714, when it was referred to as an alehouse run by a landlady called 'Big Lizzie'. It has been considerably altered since, and today looks rather like a suburban bungalow. The inn is said to be haunted by a black woman who formerly stayed at a big house nearby. Many people claim to have spotted her at the bar, or looking down from a window to the roadway below. There have also been inexplicable goings on at the inn, from cash registers opening by themselves to objects mysteriously moving from place to place – on one occasion a table somehow managed to be laid when no one was present.

Further south the village of Crawford is attractively situated in the upper reaches of Clydesdale, but for a number of years it has been bypassed by the A74 (now the M74), and its inns no longer benefit from the passing trade that they once had. The Old Post Horn Inn, a former coaching inn built in 1744, was advertised as Scotland's most haunted house when it was put on the market in 1994. This may have put prospective purchasers off, for at the time of writing it stands forlorn and empty, succumbing to the elements. Three ghosts have made their presence felt here – a young girl who was supposedly knocked down by a coach, another who is said to have been hanged for stealing a loaf of bread, and a coachman who died in a snow storm in 1805.

Although the Crawford Inn in the same village has no claims to be haunted, there is a tale associated with it which is perhaps worth relating. The inn was at one time owned by the Cranston family, operators of the last mail-coach in the area, and when one of the family died towards the end of the nineteenth century a stone obelisk was commissioned to be erected over the grave in the parish kirkyard. However, a family quarrel erupted over the tombstone, which was never erected in its rightful place. Instead it was put up at the north end of the village (actually nearer the Old Post Horn) at the junction of roads; it still stands there today.

In Glasgow – at 37 Saltmarket, one of the oldest parts of the city – is a small public house known as Graham's Bar. This is said to be haunted by a little old woman who wears a drab-coloured shawl pulled tightly over her head and round her face, hiding her features. It is thought that she may have been a former resident of the area, from the time when this was a popular residential location. This apparition has been seen a number of times by the staff of the bar, though her appearances are irregular.

The little village of Fintry nestles between the Fintry Hills and Campsie Fells. Here the Fintry Inn, which dates from 1750, is haunted by some form of ghost. According to the proprietors, many visitors have reported being visited by some form of apparition, but no-one seems to know who the earthly person may have been, or why their spirit still frequents the inn.

The Coylet Inn, on the shores of Loch Eck in Argyll, is haunted by a 'blue boy' who was drowned in the loch here. He was staying at the inn with his parents but was prone to sleep-walking and walked into the loch. When his corpse was found the following day it was blue with cold. His spirit is still said to walk through the inn, searching for his mother.

At Broadford on the Island of Skye stands the Broadford Hotel, an old two-and-a-half storey corbie-stepped building on the edge of the village. A number of guests have experienced what is usually described as a 'mist' in some of the rooms here, and others have felt some form of 'presence' around them. On a few occasions the spirit of what is thought to have been a former housekeeper at the hotel has been seen, supposedly searching for her favourite chair. An apparition has been noted on the stairs and some folk have witnessed ladders and lamps moving of their own accord.

Cameron's Inn in Aberdeen is a former coaching inn that still had the stables and cobbled courtyard until the 1970s. It was built at the end of the eighteenth century in the traditional Aberdeenshire style, with granite walls and slate roofs (though these have been altered over the years). Here sounds have been heard from empty rooms, and a cleaner once experienced something abnormal. At times there is a sudden drop in temperature in parts of the inn.

At the foot of Pannanich Hill, near Ballater on Deeside, stands the Pannanich Wells Hotel, described by Queen Victoria as a 'curious little old inn'; her ghillie, John Brown, once worked here as a stable-lad. This inn dates from 1760 and grew in popularity when taking the chalybeate waters of the Pannanich Well was regarded as a cure for various ailments. A Grey Lady haunts the building and the immediate vicinity of the hotel. At times only the sound of the spirit is heard, or else the echo of furniture being moved or doors being opened. One of the most haunted parts of the building seems to be Room Number One, where a weird smell and sounds of breathing have been experienced.

A number of strange sounds have been heard at the Moncreiffe Arms in Bridge of Earn, from crying children in empty rooms to the noise of splashing water in vacant bathrooms. At Cupar in Fife the Royal Hotel, dating from around 1835, stands on the site of a graveyard associated with a former monastery. This perhaps explains the ghostly monk that some people claim to have seen. On other occasions objects have been seen moving by themselves.

In Edinburgh's Royal Mile is Whistle Binkie's, the cellars of which are haunted by a spirit known as 'The Watcher': a male figure from the seventeenth century. This pub is regularly visited by one of the 'ghost tours' that make their way round Edinburgh, and the inn seems to keep the tourists happy. A sketch was made of the figure when he appeared in 1994, and he has manifested many times since, with dozens of people claiming to have seen him. Others have experienced a 'mist' in the cellars, and various inexplicable noises have been heard. In the bar upstairs, various weird occurrences have taken place, from oranges slicing themselves in half to clocks regularly stopping mysteriously at 4.15 a.m.

The Cross Keys Inn in Northgate, Peebles, was erected in 1693 as the town house of the Williamsons of Cardrona, their initial W being picked out in the slates on the roof. Later converted to an inn, the oldest in Peebles, it was originally named the Yett Inn (after the arched gateway through the town wall) but was later renamed the Cross Keys. This inn is full of tales. It is haunted by a former landlady, Marion Ritchie, who makes an appearance at fairly regular intervals; the inn-sign in the courtyard depicts her, and bears the inscription 'Ye came, ye went, but I hive steyed fir three hunder years'. Sir Walter Scott, who was a regular visitor to the Cross Keys, featured the inn in various novels, most notably in *St Ronan's Well*, where he bases a major character, Meg Dodds, on Marion Ritchie; in the tale the hostelry is called the Cleikum Inn. Marion Ritchie was noted for her attention to her guests. The Tweeddale Presbytery regularly dined there after their meetings. Miss Ritchie died on 8 February 1822 on one such afternoon, and her last words are said to have been, 'Are the ministers a' richt?' She had remained single all her life, having turned down offers of marriage from 'three topping farmers, two bonnet-lairds [yeomen] and a horse-couper'.

A Grey Lady haunts the Traquair Arms at Innerleithen. This inn dates from around 1836, when it was a coaching stop by the name of Riddells, but it has been extended since. The Grey Lady only appears in the original section of the building, and she has only ever been seen from the back. She wears a long grey dress with a large bustle, and her hair is tied up in a bun; who she was, or from which period, no-one knows. At Denholm, near Hawick, in the nineteenth-century Cross Keys Inn, a spirit named Harry is said to frequent the cellars and has been confirmed by a visiting clairvoyant.

Some inns have tales behind their names. In the parish of Leuchars, in north-east Fife, is a tiny hamlet called Pickletillum, named after its old inn. Situated beside the A92, three miles from the Tay Road Bridge, the inn is white-painted, with black door and window surrounds, and red shingles. Some say the name is derived from *Pette Talamh* ('portion of fine land') or Pittentulloch ('hollow under the hillock'), but there is a tale which gives another reason for it. Many years ago, perhaps in the mid-eighteenth century, a joiner working on a house ran short of nails and sent his apprentice to the nearby blacksmith to get some more. The smith did not have nails of the right size, but he had some that were quite close to what was wanted, so he told the boy just to 'Tak' a pickle till 'him' (take a few to him). It is said that the joiner was then nicknamed 'Pickletillum', and that gradually the area where he lived came to be known by the same name, which was adopted by the inn when it opened.

The Oakbank Inn, at Turret Bridge in Crieff, is well named, for it stands beside an ancient oak tree. The locals call this Eppie Callum's Tree after an early owner. Eppie did exist, but whether the tale asociated with her is true is not known. According to the locals, she planted an acorn in an old teapot which she had in the kitchen. The seed germinated and began to grow, and Eppie placed the plant in its pot on the window-sill of the inn. Within a few years it had become so big that there was insufficient room for its roots, and they began to poke through the spout, in the search for nourishment. Eppie saw this and decided that it was time to replant the tree in the garden of the inn. The tree is still growing; today it is of considerable girth and height, and probably in excess of two or three hundred years old. (The tale of Eppie has a few flaws, for the Eppie Callum recorded in history lived at a later period than the time when the tree would have been in its infancy. In her day, too, tea was such an expensive and rare luxury that she would be unlikely to own a teapot. Nevertheless, the tale survives, and the inn sign sports a large oak tree growing from a teapot.) The Oakbank Inn was a popular refreshment spot when the locality around the Turret Bridge was used for fairs and markets. An earlier landlord, Duncan (or 'Donald') Baine, was noted for his special cold punch, much loved by the Highlanders who walked many a mile to the fairs.

The Cross Keys Tavern in Edinburgh is no longer in existence, but it played an important part in the history of Scotland (we have already mentioned it in connection with the Covenanters). It used to stand in Covenant Close, south of the High Street, and was at one time run by Patrick Steill. In 1695 an Act of Scots Parliament proposing the formation of the Bank of Scotland decreed that the subscription book for shareholders (or 'adventurers', as they were styled) had to be kept in a 'publick place'. The spot chosen by the bank's Foundation Committee was the Cross Keys, and the first subscriber was the Marquis of Tweeddale, who subscribed £4000 Scots. The book opened on 1 November 1695 and remained open to subscribers for two months; 140 people signed their name in the book, and a capital of £1,200,000 Scots (£100,000 Sterling) was raised to start the bank in business. The first office was opened in 1696 and the Bank of Scotland has not looked back since.

The Inver Hotel, two miles west of Crathie on Deeside, dates from around 1760 and is distinguished by its unique chimneys, made from granite blocks. In a garden nearby lies the Inver Stone, a large boulder used in days gone by as a test of strength. (A number of these stones survive in various places throughout Scotland and are generally known as 'testing' or 'lifting stones'.) The Inver Stone weighs 265 lb, this figure being carved into it. At one time the stone was in demand at various Highland Games and was taken from Inver to the games and back. Since the Royal family acquired Balmoral Castle in 1853, the inn-keeper and staff, as well as any guests, have stood in front of the Inver hotel to wave and cheer as the royal entourage passes en route to the highland games at Braemar on the first Saturday in September.

Another Deeside hotel has two lifting stones. The Potarch Inn, near Kincardine O'Neil, dates from 1812, being built at the same time as the Potarch Bridge over the Dee, and for many years a market held here drew a large crowd. At the bridge lie the two Dinnie Stones. These were not traditional lifting stones, for they were originally used to tie up the horses of travellers who came to the hotel for a refreshment; the iron rings on their tops were primarily for this purpose, but they also came in handy for lifting them. The stones weigh 435 lb and 340 lb, and are named after a former mason in the district, Donald Dinnie (1837–1916), who could lift both at the same time – in fact, he was able to carry them the length of the bridge. After Dinnie's death the stones lay unlifted from that time until 1972, when Jack Shanks managed to equal the feat.

Outside the Loch Ericht Hotel at Dalwhinnie in Inverness-shire is another lifting stone, though this is not its traditional site. It used to lie at a nearby farm, but when this was abandoned the stone was taken to the hotel. Like the Inver Stone, this boulder (which weighs around 140 lb) was in demand at the local highland games, in this case at Newtonmore. A local games expert, George Cameron, used to carry the stone into the hotel and place it on the bar as a joke.

Today noted as a hotel for fishermen, the Altnaharra Inn, at the head of Loch Naver, has a history that belies its present image. Sutherland was noted for its clearances in the nineteenth century, when thousands of people were forced to leave their homes and find new places to live, either on the coast or in distant lands, such as North America. During one of the clearances in 1816 the old church at Achadh an Eas, at the foot of the loch, was destroyed and its main timbers were taken to Altnaharra, where they were used to build the inn; an old woman who revisited the glen after the clearances cried that, 'I have seen the timbers of our church covering the inn'. The inn was extended in 1832, when corbie-stepped gables were added, and enlarged again around 1900.

The Stair Inn, in the clachan of the same name east of Ayr, also has a tenuous link with a church. At one time the parish kirk suffered from a leaking roof, and Sunday services were held in the bar. After the sermon the congregation was given a complimentary glass of ale, and it is said that the church had its best attendance at this time! The Stair Inn, which is thought to date from around 1670, was known to Robert Burns, and he probably visited it on occasion, for it stands within striking distance of both Mauchline and Tarbolton.

At the north-eastern extremity of the mainland of Great Britain is the celebrated headland of John o' Groats, 873 miles from Land's End at the opposite corner of our island. Many people like to visit both places, and in the late nineteenth century this notion was seized upon when a hotel for visitors was built near the place where the original house of John o' Groat had stood. Jan de Groot was one of several Dutch brothers who settled here in the fifteenth century and operated a ferry to Orkney (a John Grot held a one pennyland of ground at Duncansby from the Earl of Caithness in 1496). When they all met together he and his relatives argued over who was to be seated at the head of the table, so, fed up with the squabbling, he built an eight-sided house that contained an octagonal table – which prevented anybody claiming to be seated at the head. John o' Groat died around 1509 and was buried in Canisbay churchyard, where an ancient gravestone can still be seen. It bears the inscription: *Donald Grot, sone to Johne Grot, laid me heir April XIII day 1568*. John o' Groat's house stood for many years, and was converted into an inn. It was replaced by the present John o' Groat's House Hotel, which includes an octagonal tower, in 1875–6, but the site of the original house is marked with a low mound on which stands a flagstaff.

In Anstruther Wester, in Fife, the old coaching inn named the Dreel Tavern was erected in the sixteenth century or thereabouts, though it has been much modernized since. A plaque on the wall records an incident which took place when the inn must have been fairly new:

> James V, 1513–42, travelled incognito through Fife as the 'Guid Man o' Ballengeich', coming to the Dreel Burn and fearful of wetting his hose, he was carried across at this point by a stout gaberlunzie woman, who was rewarded with the King's Purse.

A later monarch also spent a night incognito at a Scots inn on 20 September 1861. A booking was made at the Ramsay Arms Hotel (formerly the Eagle Inn) at Fettercairn for a 'marriage party from Aberdeen', and the staff were surprised to find that the party consisted of Queen Victoria and Prince Albert, along with Princess Alice, Prince Louis of Hesse and others. The Queen and her party had travelled from Balmoral by way of Invermark and Glen Esk to Fettercairn, a distance of forty miles, in what the Queen termed a 'Great Expedition.' In her journal, the Queen wrote:

> we got out at a quiet little inn, 'Ramsay Arms', quite unobserved, and went at once upstairs. There was a very nice drawing-room, and next to it a dining-room, both very clean and tidy – then to the left, our bedroom, which was excessively small, but also very clean and neat, and much better furnished than at Grantown.... The landlord and landlady knew exactly who we were, but no one else except the coachman, and they kept the secret admirably.

The hotel has been considerably extended since 1861; the room in which the royal party dined is now a drawing room, but the Queen's bedroom survives upstairs (the hangings from the bed are now in the Glenesk Folk Museum in Glen Esk, Angus). In 1864, to commemorate the visit of the royal party to the village, a large triumphal archway was built across the street, adjacent to the Ramsay Arms. Gothic in style, it is inscribed with the date and 'Victoria'. It cost almost £250 to construct.

In August 1848 the Queen and Prince Albert stayed at the Royal George Hotel in Perth; the Queen is said to have been impressed with the standard of hospitality. They 'took the four children in our carriage and drove straight to the 'George Inn', where we had the same rooms that we had last time,' according to her journal. The Queen's first visit to the George (in 1845) had been unplanned. The Queen and her family had planned to sail from Aberdeen to London after a holiday at Balmoral, but rough seas prevented this, and the journey had to be made overland. When the royal party arrived at the George Inn the management had to borrow cutlery and certain other conveniences, but the Queen nevertheless enjoyed her stay and allowed the inn to be renamed the Royal George. The Queen also gave her custom to the Royal Hotel at Comrie, a two-and-a-half-storey building where she changed horses in 1842. Queen Juliana of the Netherlands also stayed here, and other notable guests have included Lloyd George and Sara Bernhardt.

In Grantown on Spey the Grant Arms Hotel stands in the small town's Square. Queen Victoria and Prince Albert stayed here on another of their incognito tours of the Highlands in 1860. According to the Queen's journal:

We went up a small staircase, and were shown to our bedroom at the top of it – very small, but clean, with a large four-posted bed which nearly filled the whole room. Opposite was the drawing and dining-room in one, very tidy and well sized. Then came the room where Albert dressed, which was very small.... The dinner was very fair, and all very clean; soups, hodge-podge, mutton broth, with vegetables, which I did not much relish, fowl with white sauce, good roast lamb, very good potatoes, besides one or two other dishes which I did not taste, ending with a good tart of cranberries.

Wednesday, September 5. – A misty, rainy morning. Had not slept very soundly. We got up rather early, and sat working and reading in the drawing-room till the breakfast was ready, for which we had to wait some little time. Good tea and bread and butter, and some excellent porridge. Jane Shackle (who was very useful and attentive) said that they had all supped together – namely, the two maids, and Grant, Brown, Stewart and Walker (who was still there), and were very merry in the 'commercial room'.

The Imperial Hotel in Aberdeen's Stirling Street was built in 1881 specifically to be a first-class hotel. Its luxury attracted many notable clients, including Prince Alfred, Duke of Edinburgh, Prince and Princess Christian and Duke Leopold. A contemporary account says that the hotel was 'entirely removed from the disturbing influence of the railway and the dangerous and deleterious effect of proximity to the smoke and steam of the trains'. Italian Gothic in style, it was designed by James Souttar and William Henderson.

The future Napoleon III of France stayed at the Abington Hotel in the village of the same name in 1839. Prince Louis Napoleon, as he was at the time, spent a day shooting grouse on the upper Clydesdale moors before retiring to the inn, where the simple wooden chair on which he sat is still preserved, with a plaque fixed to it. The Prince was en route to the Eglinton Tournament – a magnificent yet disastrous spectacle celebrating the ancient sport of jousting, which, because of its scale and expense (combined with unceasing rain) resulted in the financial ruin of the Earl of Eglinton who organized it.

* * *

Further down Clydesdale, in Bloomgate, Lanark, is the Clydesdale Hotel, built in 1792 as the New Inn. On 20 and 21 August 1803 William and Dorothy Wordsworth and Samuel Taylor Coleridge spent the night. The hotel was built on the site of the Grey Friar's (Franciscan) monastery, founded by King Robert the Bruce in the 1320s, and its beer cellars are said to have been part of the monastery's crypt. A ghostly monk, known as the Grey Abbot, is said to haunt the hotel, though his presence is usually felt rather than seen, and in the cellars inexplicable occurrences take place, with glasses rattling and doors slamming. The ghost is said to be a friendly spirit, which looks after the hotel. A second spirit that haunts the Clydesdale is more often witnessed in the rooms near the attic. It is said that some time in the nineteenth century a young girl was asphyxiated in a fire at the hotel, and her spirit still frequents the building. Residents have noted the sound of a crying child, even when there are known to be no children in the building.

Gretna Green is famous for its runaway marriages. Scots marriage law was, and remains, less strict than that of England, and because Gretna was the first place across the border that many eloping couples reached, thousands of marriage ceremonies were performed there. England tightened up its laws relating to marriage in 1754, raising the age for marrying without parental consent to 21, and from then onwards Gretna Green became a magnet for eloping couples. In Scots law a couple could marry at sixteen without their parents' permission, and all that was required was two witnesses – no minister or vicar. Many notable people tied the knot at Gretna, among them John Peel (the huntsman), a Sicilian Prince, Italian Duke, the 10th Earl of Westmorland, the 10th Earl of Dundonald and Lord Chancellor Erskine. (Even today weddings at Gretna Green still evoke images of romance, and the registrar's office is one of the country's busiest.) The old blacksmith's shop is the place most often associated with these marriages, with the smith performing the ceremony over the anvil – but there is no proof that this was ever the case! The three main places for weddings were the Kings Head Inn in the village of Springfield, the Sark Toll Bar and Gretna Hall.

The oldest of these was the Kings Head Inn, on the old main road into Scotland from Longtown. Weddings here were performed by a 'priest' named David Laing from the 1780s onward. The innkeeper took his cut from the fee for the ceremony, and many newly-weds decided to spend their honeymoon at his hostelry. A second inn in the village used the services of Joseph Paisley, who between 1756 and 1814 also performed marriages at Gretna itself, where he had something of a monopoly. On average he married sixty couples a year, which brought him an income of £945. Paisley was a very large man, weighing 25 stones, and was noted for his ability to take vast quantities of drink and for his mighty strength – which he demonstrated by straightening out horseshoes with his bare hands.

In 1830 the new 'English Road' was built, which took a more direct line from Carlisle to Gretna, crossing the Esk at Metalbridge. This road entered Gretna at a new toll house on the river Sark, known as Sark Toll Bar, which now became the first house in Scotland. Here Simon Beattie, and later John Murray, performed marriages, and a sign over the door today proclaims:

Over 10,000 Marriages performed in this Marriage Room, Estd. 1830.

The King's Head became a less popular place for marriages after 1830.

In 1825 Gretna Hall was leased by John Linton and converted into a hotel. He arranged for coach parties to stop there, and provided a quality service which included marriages. Charles Dickens, who visited in 1852, noted some of the graffiti on the wall of the inn – including – 'John Anderson made a fool of himself at Gretna 1831'. At the Toll Inn in the village, 1,300 marriages were conducted over a period of six years.

The marriage laws were changed in 1856 when the Lord Chancellor Lord Brougham's Act required a period of residence in Scotland before couples could be married under Scots law. He must have had some reason for wanting to end the practice – he was known to have been a Gretna bridegroom himself!

A tale of love is associated with the Cross Keys Inn at Douglas in upper Clydesdale. The inn still boasts a fireplace over which is a panel dated 1690 bearing the initials CC and NV, to commemorate Catherine Cranstoun and her husband, who built the inn and ran it for many years. Catherine Cranstoun was a lady of noble birth from the district who lived for a time in France; she caused much gossip and scandal when she eloped with her coachman and set up home here.

At Turriff, an old farming village set in the heart of the Buchan countryside, the L-shaped Fife Arms Hotel in the square at the top of the town was the scene of a famous incident in 1913. A local farmer, Robert Paterson of Lendrum, refused to pay Lloyd George's newly-introduced National Insurance contributions for employees. He was fined, but refused to pay the arrears due, so the Sheriff's Officers impounded his best white cow in order to sell it and pay the fine from the proceeds. The sale took place in the Fife Arms, and the local farm labourers were granted a half-day holiday so that they could attend. Paterson had painted a slogan on the cow – *LG & Coo, Lendrum to Leeks* – which the Sheriff's Officers removed with turpentine. But the smell of turpentine made the cow restless, and it stormed about the sale until its unease infected the labourers who began to riot and throw things at the auctioneer and sheriff. Eight people, including Paterson, were arrested and tried for inciting a riot and preventing the sale of the cow, but the case was found Not Proven, and they were released. The cow, which had meanwhile been successfully sold at Aberdeen, was bought back by a group of Buchan farmers and returned to Lendrum. Known as the Turra Coo, it was commemorated by a memorial at the farm and by china models still on sale in the town.

At Cambus o' May, near Ballater on Deeside, stands a roadside cottage that was formerly the Old Ferry Inn. The building, which was formerly thatched and is thought to be two centuries old, was originally a droving inn and later a coaching stop. (The ferry after which it is named crossed the River Dee, but a footbridge made the boat redundant.) The building is of interest, however, for the corner that was cut off it to allow the old Deeside railway to pass by. The road and river make their way through a narrow pass here, and when the railway was being built in 1863 the Marquis of Huntly refused to sell the necessary land, so a back corner of the building was removed, and a new wall built at an angle, producing a chamfered corner. The railway has long-since been closed, but the old inn – now known as Cut-a-Way Cottage – survives, visible to travellers on the north Deeside road.

On the Island of Seil in Argyll – which is reached dry-shod by crossing the 'Bridge over the Atlantic', or Clachan Bridge – is the inn known in Gaelic as Tigh an Truish (the 'house or hotel of the trousers'). It gets its name from the time when Highland dress was forbidden by law after the defeat of the second Jacobite rebellion at the Battle of Culloden in 1746. Anyone caught wearing the kilt, or any tartan clothing, was regarded as being a follower of Prince Charles, but the people of Seil decided to ignore the law and go about their daily life dressed in the traditional manner. However, when they had to travel to the mainland, they stopped at this inn and changed into trousers; their kilts were kept under lock and key by the landlord, to be picked up on their return. A contradictory version of the tale relates that, whilst kilts and tartan were proscribed, it was permissible to wear them if on service in one of His Majesty's regiments that had the kilt as part of its uniform. Soldiers returning from the mainland would stop at Tigh an Truish and change into trousers on their return from service.

At the beginning of the nineteenth century a disturbance took place at the Buck's Head Inn (now renamed the Glaisnock Inn) in Cumnock. A meeting of local farmers was held in this red sandstone building on 10 June 1833 to discuss how best to deal with a spate of serious poaching in the district. The poachers heard of the meeting and throughout the evening kept disturbing the meeting. At length the farmers threatened them with their shotguns, saying that 'the first man who opened the meeting room door once again would be shot'. When David Reid, one of their own members, arrived late for the meeting things had got so bad that he was shot before he was recognized!

At Strathmiglo in Fife the Strathmiglo Inn has a public right of way running through the building. Over a doorway leading to a passageway is a sign announcing that there is a twenty-four hour right of access through the close to the Back Dykes.

At Moffat James Duncan, a merchant in the town, built the four-storey Annandale Arms in around 1752 – though it is said that the masons he employed were lured away to work on nearby Moffat House by the promise of an extra penny a day, over and above their current wage of eightpence a day. This inn was originally known as the King's Arms and was regarded as the 'head inn' of the town and a major stopping point for mail-coaches and travellers; at the back it had stabling for fifty horses. In the winter of 1775 MacCulloch of Ardwell and the actor Samuel Foote, deterred by drifting snow and blizzard conditions on the wild road over Ericstane Brae, turned back and spent the night at the King's

Arms, then run by a Mrs Little. As the evening progressed, and things got increasingly convivial, Foote managed to acquire Mrs Little's dress and other items of her clothing. These he donned, and gave an impersonation so good that the puzzled servants never doubted that it was the landlady herself who was giving them strange orders! In 1817 the Grand Duke Nicholas of Russia stayed at the King's Arms and was so pleased with the service provided by the landlord, a Mr Robinson, that he paid him double the amount on the bill. Another notable visitor was an Austrian prince.

The King's Arms at this time had a great reputation among travellers, but all was to change. When the new road through Evandale and over the Beattock Summit to Elvanfoot was finished in 1808, a new inn was opened at Beattock. This was paid for as public accommodation by the Treasury and was 'kept in a superior and most satisfactory manner by a respectable family, who came from England'. The loss of trade to this inn, as well as to the Spur Inn (now the Balmoral Hotel), which opened in Moffat in 1800, eventually led to the King's Arms being converted into rooms and kitchens for poorer inhabitants. The tide turned in its favour again, however, when the

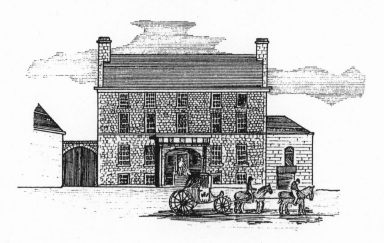

Annandale Arms Hotel, Moffat

proprietors of the Spur, the Cranstoun family, acquired the King's Arms, refitted it and renamed it the Annandale Arms; Mrs Cranstoun remained as proprietrix until 1863.

The Beehive Inn in Edinburgh's Grassmarket occupies a building dating from 1867–8 and designed by the noted architect, John Paterson. But this stands on the site of an earlier building, said to have been built in or around 1500, that had been a coaching inn, much frequented by those who came to the large market that used to be held in the street here. Over the door of the present building is a stone representation of a beehive, and the inn contains a number of ancient relics – among them a fifteenth-century wrought-iron grate in the dining room. There is also a more gruesome relic: the door to the 'condemned cell' from the old Calton gaol.

Another old Edinburgh inn is Ye Olde Golf Tavern on the edge of Bruntsfield Links. This park extends to 35 acres and was at one time part of the Burgh Muir, gifted to the city in 1508 by James VI. Here the sport of golf was at one time played (the links was one of the earliest known courses), but, as the land around the park was developed it became too cramped, and the courses were moved elsewhere. The Olde Golf Tavern still remains, though. It is claimed that the inn was first established in 1456, though the present sandstone building is much later, dating from the early nineteenth century and altered in 1899 by R.M. Cameron. It is said that part of the adjoining building, which was formerly part of the inn, dates from 1717.

In the High Street of Peebles stands the Tontine Hotel; set back from the street line, it dates from 1808. It was erected at a cost of over £4000 and initially financed on the tontine system. This is a method under which a group of shareholders jointly invests in a project, but when any member of the group dies his share is split between the surviving members, thus increasing their holding; the last survivor (in this case Sir John Hay of Haystoun) becomes the sole proprietor. The Tontine Hotel was erected partly with labour supplied by French prisoners-of-war. Its exterior is finished in the traditional Scots Georgian manner – white-painted with black door and window surrounds – and the dining room has a musicians' gallery. According to Slater's *Directory*, the landlord of this 'posting-house' in 1867 was one John Smith. At the rear there is a modern extension overlooking the Tweed.

The Tweeddale Shooting Club regularly meet in the Tontine (one of its rooms is now named the Tweeddale Shoot Bar). This is the oldest sporting club in Great Britain. In 1790 a shoot had been organized by Walter Williamson of Cardrona, to which local gentry were invited. They afterwards went to the Cross Keys in Peebles for a meal, and it was there that the club was founded. Among the original members were Lord Elibank, Sir James Naesmyth of Posso, James Wolfe Murray of Cringletie and Williamson of Cardrona. The club rules dictate that there should be no more than thirty members, and that they attend its meetings dressed in a dark green uniform. The club formed its own collection of wines, and these were moved with the club to the Tontine in 1808, where a cellar for the sole use of the club survives. In 1822 Mr Paterson of Braithwood presented a ram's-horn snuff-mull decorated with silver ornaments, which is still used at all formal occasions. The club originally held three dinners per annum, for the grouse, partridge and pheasant seasons, but this has been reduced to two.

At Kirk Yetholm in the Border countryside near Kelso stands the Border Hotel. The oldest part, half-timbered and still retaining its thatched roof, dates from the seventeenth century, when the inn was known as the Nag's Head. The inn has since been considerably extended in a similar style but with the roof covered in pantiles. Yetholm was at one time famous for its gypsies, and the 'palace' of the 'King' of the gypsies (little more than a tiny cottage) survives. The landlord at the Nag's Head would not allow the gypsies to enter his hostelry, but being a shrewd man, he realized that he might be missing some important trade. Next to the inn's doorway he made a hatch through the wall to which gypsies could come and be served ale 'to carry away'. The hatch still survives, but has been converted into a letter box. The Border Hotel is the northern terminus of the Pennine Way long-distance footpath, which runs for 250 miles from Edale in the Derbyshire Peak District. Alfred Wainwright, the famous Lakeland guidebook-writer, had an arrangement that anyone completing the walk with one of his guidebooks could get a free half-pint at the hotel – but sadly, since his death, this no longer applies. The inn has a number of Wainwright's etchings on display.

The Balnagown Arms in the market square of Ardgay at the head of the Dornoch Firth had a boulder of white quartzite, known as Clach Eiteag, built into an outside wall. This stone was used to mark the local Féill Éiteagan ('Fair of St Eitachan') that was at one time held at Alltnacealgach on Loch Borralan in western Sutherland. The location of the fair seems to have been bound up with that of the stone, the fair having to be held wherever the stone was. The people of the eastern half of the county wanted to have the fair nearer to them, so the stone was stolen and transferred to Strath Oykel, twelve miles or so to the east. But the stone did not settle, for the people of Invershin, another dozen miles eastwards, decided that it would be advantageous to have the fair there. The outcry in the district was tremendous, and heated discussions and arguments raged over where the stone, and thus the fair, should be held. At length the local laird, Ross of Balnagown, had to intervene. He chose a fourth location, in a more populous spot readily reached from all parts of Sutherland and Ross; he also instructed that the stone be built into the wall of the Balnagown Arms so that it could not be stolen again. Thus the market was for years held at Ardgay, though it has died off in modern times. The stone is now mounted in the centre of the village.

At Fairmilehead, on the outskirts of Edinburgh, stands the

Hunter's Tryst, an old inn dating from the late eighteenth century but extensively rebuilt since that time. In the early years of the nineteenth century this was the home of the 'Six Foot Club', an exclusive group of men six foot or more in height. Among the members were notable literati, including Sir Walter Scott, James Hogg and Professor John Wilson ('Christopher North').

The Ardeonaig Hotel is a small and remote wayside inn on the south side of Loch Tay. The name is pronounced 'Ar-joanig', and the inn dates from the middle of the seventeenth century. The site is an ancient one, however, and the rear wall of the inn has a baptismal font built into it; this probably came from the nearby ruined church of St Adamnan. The inn is known in Gaelic as *Tigh na Linne* ('house of the pool'), a name derived from the time when a band of raiders were ambushed by the local chieftain and his followers as they were fording the Ardeonaig Burn. The raiders' piper was killed by an arrow as he crossed the pool.

Ardeonaig Hotel, Loch Tay

Bibliography

Beveridge, David, *Between the Ochils and the Forth* (William Blackwood, 1888)

Black's Picturesque Tourist (A & C Black, 1882)

Boswell, James, *Journal of a Tour to the Hebrides* (Charles Dilly, 1785)

Brown, Peter Hume, *Early Travellers in Scotland* (David Douglas, 1891)

Burt, Edward, *Letters from a Gentleman in the North of Scotland to his Friend in England* (London, 1754)

Carlyle, Dr Alexander, *Autobiography* (London, 1860)

Chambers, Robert, *Traditions of Edinburgh* (Chambers, 1824)

Cockburn, Lord, *Circuit Journeys* (David Douglas, 1888)

Cooper, Derek, *Road to the Isles* (Routledge & Kegan Paul, 1979)

Fraser, George Milne, *The Old Deeside Road* (Aberdeen NH&AS, 1921)

Gordon, Anne, *To Move With the Times* (Aberdeen University Press, 1988)

Graham, Henry G., *Social Life in Scotland in the Eighteenth Century* (A & C Black, 1901)

Grant of Rothiemurchus, Elizabeth, *Memoirs of a Highland Lady* (John Murray, 1898)

Haldane, A.R.B., *The Drove Roads of Scotland* (Edinburgh University Press, 1952)
New Ways Through the Glens (Edinburgh University Press, 1962)
Three Centuries of Scottish Posts (Edinburgh University Press, 1971)

Hogg, James, *Highland Tours, 1803–4* (Byway Books, 1981)

HRH Queen Victoria, *Leaves from the Journal of Our Life in the Highlands* (1848–61)

Johnson, Dr Samuel, *A Journey to the Western Islands* (Strahan & Cadell, 1775)

Kenna, Rudolph, & Mooney, Anthony, *People's Palaces: Victorian and Edwardian Pubs of Scotland* (Paul Harris, 1983)

Taylor, William, *The Military Roads in Scotland* (David & Charles, 1976)

Mitchell, Joseph, *Reminiscences of My Life in the Highlands* (1884)

Pennant, Thomas, *A Tour in Scotland* (Benjamin White, 1799)

Salmond, J.B., *Wade in Scotland* (Moray Press, 1934)

Scott, Sir Walter, *Guy Mannering* (William Blackwood, 1829)

Smith, Alexander, *A Summer in Skye* (1835)

Southey, Robert, *Journal of a Tour in Scotland in 1819* (1929)

Stevenson, Robert Louis, *Kidnapped* (1886)

Stuart, Marie W., *Old Edinburgh Taverns* (Edinburgh, 1952)

Teignmouth, Baron, *Sketches of the Coasts and Islands* (London, 1836)

Wordsworth, Dorothy, *Recollections of a Tour in Scotland in 1803* (David Douglas, 1874)

In the course of research, the author has also referred to numerous local guidebooks, old and new, newspapers and magazines of various periods, notably the *Glasgow Herald* and *Scots Magazine*, Scottish Tourist Board information, tourist leaflets, inn and hotel brochures, questionnaires completed by many innkeepers, and 'on the spot' investigations, in the compilation of this book.

Index